Copyright © 2020 by Jackson Leonard

Gregg Troy - It's Never Easy
Leadership, Swimming, and the Value of Challenging Work

Author: Jackson Leonard
Contributing Authors: Gregg Troy, Ryan Lochte, Caeleb Dressel
Editor: Marla McKenna
Associate Editor: Griffin Mill
Proofreader: Lyda Rose Haerle
Cover Design: Jackson Leonard
Cover and Interior Layout: Michael Nicloy

Front cover photo courtesy of Jack Spitser Photography
Back cover photo courtesy of the University Athletic Association, UF

ISBN: 978-1945907593

Published by Nico 11 Publishing & Design | Mukwonago, Wisconsin
Michael Nicloy, Publisher
www.nico11publishing.com

Be well read.

Quantity order requests can be emailed to the Publisher:
mike@nico11publishing.com

Printed in The United States of America

GREGG TROY

It's Never Easy

*Leadership, Swimming, and
the Value of Challenging Work*

By Jackson Leonard
With U.S. Olympic Head Swimming Coach Gregg Troy
and Olympic Gold Medalists, Ryan Lochte, and Caeleb Dressel

TABLE OF CONTENTS

"If you want to make everyone happy, don't be a leader. Sell ice cream."

- Steve Jobs

"Don't ever confuse motion with progress."

- Robert Louis Stevenson

"It is not the critic who counts; not the man who points out how the strong man stumbles, or where the doer of deeds could have done them better. The credit belongs to the man who is actually in the arena, whose face is marred by dust and sweat and blood; who strives valiantly; who errs, who comes short again and again, because there is no effort without error and shortcoming; but who does actually strive to do the deeds; who knows great enthusiasms, the great devotions; who spends himself in a worthy cause; who at the best knows in the end the triumph of high achievement, and who at the worst, if he fails, at least fails while daring greatly, so that his place shall never be with those cold and timid souls who neither know victory nor defeat."

- President Theodore Roosevelt

THE COACHING TREE

A sense of dread and apprehension overwhelmed me as I swiped my college ID to enter the University of Florida Swimming and Diving offices and locker rooms. I was a half an hour ahead of even the earliest varsity swimmers, who usually arrived 15 minutes early to practice, a habit of punctuality notoriously known amongst the swimmers and coaches as, "Gator Time." Anyone walking onto the pool deck five minutes before practice time officially starts has typically missed the entire explanation of the warmup and two or three key focus points for that session.

I was early to the office because I was embarrassed to be seen by my friends and former teammates, whom I had ditched a semester before. After spending nine months training with the Gators, or more accurately, *surviving* practices, I had told Head Coach Gregg Troy that I was quitting the team. Coach Troy, to his credit, had suggested I stick it out for a few more weeks and try resting and suiting up for one final meet before hanging up my suit for good. He thought a little rest and a racing suit might give me a boost at our next meet and might have allowed me to see my efforts in the last nine months hadn't been in vain. The fact was: I couldn't bear another Sunday night of dreading Monday morning practice. I couldn't bear to be run over by the older *females* in practice, never mind the other guys. I was ready to move on with my life, and I had just disappeared. Not exactly my most mature moment, I'll admit.

After spending three months hiding in my room, watching *Seinfeld* in its entirety, and eating exclusively from the dorm's vending machine, I decided to turn my life around. No more wallowing; no more self-loathing. As a starting point, it was time to get back in shape. I bought running shoes and spent the remaining weeks of the year figuring out how to run more than two miles without requiring an ambulance ride back to the dorm. By the time summer rolled around, I could skillfully avoid running past the pool (still a source of shame for me) and finish anywhere from five to 10 miles without requiring medical assistance. I headed home to South Florida after my freshman year to figure out my next steps. Then spending a summer at home teaching swim lessons and acting as a substitute swim coach sparked, what would become, my life's passion—coaching the sport of swimming.

With a summer of coaching novice swimmers under my belt, I had to adjust my upcoming semester's course load to appropriately reflect my newfound passion and purpose. What courses should I take? No need to load up on pre-med courses or biology and chemistry anymore like many freshman; I had entered school thinking I wanted to be a doctor. But now, having settled on a career path, I worried about finding work as a coach in Gainesville. The answer stared back in the form of Coach Troy's familiar mustachioed face, smiling on the cover of an *American Swimming* magazine strewn across my kitchen counter. I knew then that I would have to ask Coach Troy for help. Perhaps I could help as a team manager; I had seen guys helping out around deck while I swam. They usually only fetched goggles or did the team laundry, but that menial work would get me back on deck. To get that job, I would have to return to the pool and face my failure as a swimmer. I would have to explain how I could be of use and why I would be different as a manager.

Cautiously, I climbed the stairs in the main room to the second floor, where coaches' offices were located. In my time with the Gators as an athlete, I hadn't been in any of the offices for an extended period of time; I had always assumed the coaches had better athletes to deal with and kept my distance. Each step closer to Coach Troy's door was increasingly nerve-racking for me. *What if he's not in the office? What if I run into one of the other coaches and have to explain why I'm here? If I have to come back again, it'll be mortifying...*I could feel my heartbeat in my ears as I knocked on his door. Lacking the confidence to even walk straight into his office, I peered around the corner with apprehension. Coach Troy, glasses on and pen in hand, was scribbling the intricate notes that would become that day's workout. Columns and arrows jettisoned every which direction.

"Jackson Leonard, come in," he said, with a slight smile creeping out of one side of his mouth.

A cursory look around the room told any visitor what most swimmers already recognized—Coach Troy knew swimming. Framed *Swimming World* magazines of his former champions lined the shelving cabinets, multiple Coach of the Year awards from various organizations were hung on the white walls, and trophies and mementos from international team trips littered the many surfaces of his office. I sat down on the black leather couch across from him and sunk down to what felt like the floor. I felt my mouth go dry as I stammered and explained why I had returned. Coach Troy slowly nodded and smiled as I kept explaining my newfound desire to coach. Every time I paused to catch my breath, he would wait and just look at me. I would learn in the coming years that he often got swimmers and coaches to continue speaking by just *waiting*. He was like Dr. Phil staring at me, just waiting to hear me explain more. After several minutes of rambling, Coach Troy finally cut in and said, "Jackson, before you quit, I told you to think about quitting and come back to me to make sure it's what you really want. You didn't come back."

As my face flushed and my temples pulsed, I quietly explained the shame I felt at not being properly prepared to keep up with practices. My high school coach, a wonderful human being and gentle giant, had pushed me to be my best but hadn't challenged me to improve my technique in anything but freestyle, the most basic swimming stroke. I had decided to learn to be the best coach possible so that no one I ever coached would have to quit a college team because they hadn't been prepared well enough—technically or physically. I told Coach Troy, "I promise you. I will be better as a manager. I will work as hard as anyone you've ever seen. I just want to learn about coaching."

Coach Troy just looked at me with a long fixed gaze I would come to both fear and crave, a gaze I would avoid desperately but also eagerly seek. After what felt like an eternity, Coach Troy picked up the practice he'd just written, handed it to me, and said, "Coaches will need five copies of this, and the swimmers will need Gatorade made in the cooler on deck. The head manager can show you how to make it today. You're in charge the rest of the week." I clamored from the bottom of the couch and jumped to attention to hurry to the copier.

I didn't know it then, but Coach Troy's willingness to trust me, a mediocre walk-on who quit, would lead to a career and passion that would influence hundreds, if not thousands of others; such is the power of influence for this book's focus, Gregg Troy.

In the coaching world, every coach influences his or her swimmers and assistant coaches below them. In turn, these learned styles of coaching and methods of leadership are passed on to other swimmers and coaches. This cascade of influence creates a proverbial coaching tree. Coach Gregg Troy has one of the largest and most influential coaching trees in the history of American swimming. As a club coach, collegiate coach, international team coach, and U.S. Olympic Head Coach, his reach extends to the corners of the world and has trickled down to reach thousands of swimmers and hundreds of coaches. Below, a small sampling of coaches, administrators, and swimmers speak to the profound effect Coach Troy has had on their lives. Some of these characters we'll see again in the upcoming pages, but by no means is this list complete.

Gregg Troy is so much more than a swim coach. The man is a teacher, a leader, and an influencer. He's impacted my life as an athlete, a coach, a husband, and now as a father. His harsh truths are not for everyone, but for me those harsh truths meant he cared about me reaching my highest potential in and out of the pool. Caring and being passionate about your profession will create followers. I am without a doubt a Gregg Troy follower.

Mike Joyce
Former Gator All-American, Auburn Assistant Coach

The best way to sum up Coach Troy is he was a perfectionist. If you strived for that, then he gave you all he had. If you were not into that, then he had no time for you. His reputation came from those people he had no time for! Working for Coach Troy for 23 years set me up for my current job. Working for him was the single greatest benefit and the biggest hindrance, and it was only a hindrance because I worked in a bubble and came out expecting everyone else everywhere to work at his level of excellence. I was disappointed at what the world was really like.

> Martyn Wilby
> Swimming Canada, Former UF Women's Associate Head Coach

Gregg is a real competitor. Over the years we've had some great battles in the pool, but at the end of the day, he and I are more alike than most people realize. It was always exciting to race him and the Gators.

> Jack Bauerle
> University of Georgia Head Coach

Troy had an innate ability to read his swimmers and understood each as an individual and how to train and rest each athlete as an individual. I see it in his coaching today; he's implementing lessons learned early on in his career and I like to think I helped in a way, as I was not easy. As he has said to me many times, 'It probably is more difficult to train great athletes who are the best in the world than middle of the road athletes.' I believe that is because the great ones are always very strong willed and that can be difficult for weak coaches. Troy is as strong of a coach I know; he knows when to push and when to put his arm around you...

I love Greg with all my heart and would walk through fire for him; anytime, anyplace.

> David McCagg
> Fort Myers alumni, Former multi-time Pan American Champion, World Champion, and World Record Holder

Gregg has always been a disruptor in our industry. A disruptor changes the landscape of their craft for the better. He knows no other way. He thinks out of the box, and he drives his thoughts with a strong conviction. His conviction is the way he guides his beliefs. He has a beautiful skill in creating an off axis that tilts his coaching philosophy and a courage that requires an independent spirit. He has a very clear philosophy on who he is as a coach, and how he will conduct his life as a man is clear to everyone he works with. He has become a very good friend.

Jack Roach
Former National Junior Team Program Director at USA
Swimming and 2016 US National Team Consultant to
Athlete and Coach Relations

Coach Troy is one of the true coaching greats in the history of the sport. Few have developed champions at every level including: club, high school, college, and on the Olympic world stage.
When you look at the number of Olympic Medalists, World Champions, and World Record Holders that he has developed over the last three decades, they span a wide range of events and specialties. I think this speaks to Coach Troy's full breadth of knowledge of the sport and his innate understanding of what is necessary in each of the disciplines to reach the top of the podium.

Jeff Poppell
UF Women's Swimming Head Coach

Coach Troy is a first class coach and one of the sport's greats. I had nothing but positive experiences around him as a volunteer assistant. I found him welcoming and willing to share his opinions on almost every aspect of training. I found my time with the Gators leading into Beijing to be one of the most positive experiences of my life.

Paul Donovan
Former Head Coach at the National Aquatic Centre
Performance Centre for Swim Ireland, current Head Coach
for the Jersey Wahoos

Coach Troy was basically a second parent to me here in the States. He went above and beyond to make me feel comfortable outside of the pool, so that I could perform well in the pool and have less distractions while I was racing and training...We became friends outside of the pool after five and half years, but he said, 'I don't want to do you the disservice of turning a blind eye or not pushing you enough. So, when we get to the pool, I'm going to push you and I want you to expect that.' He wanted to be that guy who could push you. We definitely clashed and it was never a bad thing. In the heat of the moment of high training, he'd be challenging me, and I'm always thankful for doing that to me throughout my career.

Sebastian Rousseau
Florida Gator and South African Olympian ('08, '12, '16)

Gregg Troy at Florida was exactly what I needed—he was always there for me to bounce ideas off of, and he kept me honest at practice, but never overstepped his boundaries. He was not afraid to criticize, but offered praise when praise was earned. Towards the end of my career, I was an athlete who responded much better to a coach pushing me to my limit and holding me accountable, rather than constant praise.

Elizabeth Beisel,
Florida Gator, USA Olympian ('08, '12, '16 Olympic Silver Medalist) and Team USA Captain

He doesn't let you cheat yourself of what you are capable of. He's old-fashioned but at the same time never fails to plan for the future. He's like an old man whose mind lives in the future for the sake of his swimmers, always thinking, always learning, and always sharing.

Caeleb Dressel
Florida Gator, USA Olympian, Gold Medalist

He's just the world's best coach. Plain and simple.

Ryan Lochte
Florida Gator, USA Olympian, 12x Olympic Medalist

I have a tremendous amount of respect for Coach Troy. He worked his tail off. His program, at the outset, was a little like the tortoise from The Tortoise and the Hare. He was never banging on doors demanding anything. He and his staff just worked day after day, building little by little to create an amazing program. He was and is an absolute professional and that is reflected in the success he has had. He is certainly one of my favorite coaches and one of the best people I've had the pleasure of knowing.

Jeremy Foley
Former University of Florida Athletic Director (1992-2016)

CHAPTER ONE

FAMILY AND EARLY LIFE

Leadership Begins at Home: A Son Emulates His Father

A young, 17-year-old, Gregg Troy walked on to the Fort Myers Country Club pool deck and surveyed the scene. He had swum in the pool a time or two as a swimmer himself, but now he had a newfound perspective. Today was Gregg's first day on the job as the new age group coach, and he was in charge of all swimmers under the age of 15. With no formal training in coaching or education, Gregg would approach the position as most new coaches do—by emulating what their coaches did for them. He planned for a warm-up, a main set, and a cool down, but knew he would probably have to adjust since he would have differing ages and abilities all at once.

This summer job had fallen in his lap, but it was a way to make a few extra bucks and it was a topic he knew and loved, so it beat bagging groceries. Gregg himself hadn't started swimming until his best friend in middle school urged him to join the team. Now, just a few months before leaving for college, Gregg already had plans to swim at TCU and enjoyed his club team workouts. This temporary coaching gig couldn't be that hard; he'd been to a thousand practices himself! Writing a few workouts and being in the sun couldn't be difficult.

As swimmers started running and skipping in, Gregg was filled with a mixture of apprehension and excitement. It was hard to tell by now if the sweat on his brow was caused by the anxiety of being newly in charge of so many kids or if the sweltering, west Florida, mid-afternoon heat was to blame. Just as practice was supposed to begin, Gregg had a thought that would recur for years to come, *"What would Dad do?"* His father hadn't coached a day in his life, but Gregg knew to model his own behavior and demeanor based on his father's strength. Wiping the sweat from his brow, Gregg grabbed a towel, whistled loudly (hands free by folding his tongue, a skill many would come to envy), and organized swimmers into groups. He had committed to the job, nothing to do now but get started. The practices that followed were structured and fun, challenging and exciting; sometimes it felt like the coach was flying by the seat of his pants, other times there was no questioning it, Coach knew his strokes and you'd better pay attention. For the next forty years, two things would remain constant: first, Coach Troy's practices always retained that combination and mixture of discipline, challenge, excitement, and a "fly by the seat of your pants" feel, and second, he would always refer to what his father had done. For Gregg Troy, the first example of leadership and discipline, staples of the several elite training grounds he would come to put his stamp on, came from his task-driven, army-trained father, Walter Troy.

Walter's Travels

Walter Troy, the middle son of seven, had to find work. A Depression-era Dust Bowl teenager, Walter desperately needed money, as did most Americans at the time. Walter's family, middle-class laborers for the local Coca-Cola factory in rural Pennsylvania, had been hit hard by the Depression, and the loss of the family's assets meant everyone had to find work and *fast*.

Walter's plan for a better life came to him one night. The next morning, he was headed out west in search of employment. Hitchhiking west from Pennsylvania, Walter found himself en route to San Francisco. Finding transportation and free rides was no easy feat, and each stop along the route proved fruitless. After months of travel, Walter hooked up with some new friends and settled into a one-bedroom apartment in the Bay City. The four of them shared the cramped space by picking up a few odd jobs here and there. Alas, the four young men scraped together enough cash to split the apartment's rent and live under a solid roof, no small task during the Depression. Unfortunately, that was about all they could afford. As he would later tell his children, there was a time when Walter had to live on just one meal a day, if one would call a single cup of lukewarm coffee and a 10-cent donut a meal.

The challenge and the distance from home didn't phase him though. For six months Walter was able to eek out a living and make it day to day. But, alas, after half a year of the same cup of coffee and too many stale donuts to recount, Walter stuck up his thumb and started hitchhiking back home. It was time to figure out a new plan.

Service: The Pennsylvania State Troopers and World War II

Service would come to envelop Walter's life. Upon returning home from his stint out west, he studied hard and worked fastidiously in the police academy to earn a spot on the Pennsylvania State Trooper Patrol. The work was consistent. Discipline and structure were what Walter understood and appreciated. Life continued on an upward trajectory until the United States became involved in World War II.

Walter Troy (left)

Walter Troy
Photos courtesy of Kathleen Troy

While some would appreciate an excuse to not be shipped off to Europe, Walter took issue with being excluded from service. Ever the patriot, Walter and a handful of other state troopers were incensed at the mandate prohibiting them from enlisting because they "had a secure job at home." Like university students, select workers were allowed to defer draft appointments and continue their work at home. Walter was outraged that some people were passing on the draft, when he and his buddies were being barred from service. Believing they needed to serve, the group of state troopers took their complaints to the Pennsylvania state legislature and petitioned the allowance to fight the Axis powers. Different and steadfast men, Walter and his fellow troopers were granted the ability to enlist and were off in the name of patriotism Walter wound up in the Pacific arena. On his way to Australia, he shipped through a familiar port,

San Francisco. As an older enlisted man with years of work under his belt, 29-year-old Private Troy found himself in an interesting dynamic, working with much younger 19-year-olds whom he would have to connect with and lead. His time in the Pennsylvania State Police force was put to use as he was promoted and assigned behind enemy lines in the Philippines. At Leyte Gulf, Walter helped organize the Mora guerillas. When the U.S.'s top General MacArthur left the area, the Allied forces sent troops back in to organize the resistance movement. Walter was a part of that force; though in later years, he wouldn't speak much of his time spent in Southeast Asia.

Walter watched the Battle of Leyte Gulf, which annihilated and broke the Japanese Navy to the point where they were no longer a factor in the Pacific fight. That allowed General MacArthur to go back into the Philippines with minimal resistance. Private Troy was wounded in the bicep while in the Philippines and was sent back to San Francisco to recover at a U.S. military hospital. His eventual convalescence coincided with the U.S. occupation of Japan, at which point, Walter stepped into a military police role in charge of about 150 high ranking Japanese military and government officials at a prisoner of war (POW) camp.

Six months serving in the POW camp passed, and the war started winding down. The U.S. government began to pare down the armed forces to only essential jobs, which meant Walter would need to find a different path. He loved the discipline, he loved the structure, and he loved the lifestyle. Now a Captain and still unmarried, this military regimen suited Walter, but it wasn't long before the Pennsylvania Troopers started calling. They wanted him back. Walter would remain with the State police for another 25 years before retiring and moving from the dreaded cold down to the Sunshine State.

As many sons and daughters of servicemen and women will attest to, Gregg rarely heard his father talk about his days in the armed forces. Similarly, Walter didn't come home divulging all the details of every day on the highway as a Pennsylvania State Trooper. However, both positions would shape the way Walter lived, talked, and acted. Consequently, Walter's children would learn the benefits and need for developing a sense of purpose, drive, and order.

Gregg, as a Swimmer

Gregg's father never pushed the sport of swimming on him. Walter knew to allow his young son to figure out which sport to do without the pressure of an overbearing figure. As many keen and observant parents will tell you, most children will actively rebel against activities being forced upon them; true passion comes from within. A friend from school bet Gregg he couldn't finish a swim practice. Ever competitive, Gregg rose to the challenge and a little challenge can add fuel to the fire. Gregg came, survived, and enjoyed the practice! He was hooked; a little cajoling was all it took.

Aside from a year in high school swimming for John Rangeley, Gregg never swam for great swimming masterminds. His coaches were all great people, by his account, but no one was a stellar technician or very demanding at that. The problem with being coached by someone who doesn't grasp the mechanics of the strokes or by someone who cannot teach technical skills well is that swimming in water is unnatural to humans. Water doesn't stay in one place and moving through it requires the right amount of force at precisely the right angles. The coaches who know how to teach technique are the coaches who develop fast swimmers. Coaches who lack knowledge on technique will always be handicapped.

Gregg Troy as a high school senior.
Picture courtesy of Kathleen Troy

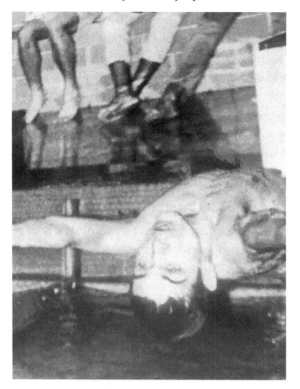

Gregg as a high school swimmer.
Picture courtesy of Kathleen Troy

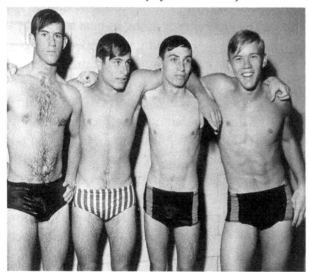

Gregg, third from left, with high school teammates.
Photo courtesy of Kathleen Troy

Gregg would work hard swimming through high school and, after graduation, landed at Texas Christian University's (TCU) rather poor swim team. With only one team answering his high school letters and recruiting calls though, Gregg was not a highly recruited athlete out of high school, and he found himself leading Rufe Brewton's Horned Frogs. Twice-daily practices were offered at TCU, but most swimmers came in with a limited swimming background and weren't capable of handling a great deal of training or volume. Coach Brewton was a Texas native, disciplined and trained to coach in the image of Bear Bryant, as most Texas coaches were at that time. Bear Bryant's legacy as a Texas football coach, and eventually a multiple-time National Champion at the University of Alabama, was considered *the* coaching model of the time. Structure and order were valued and required; these two themes would continue to follow Gregg for years.

Gregg would continue to remind athletes, his entire career, that he, himself, was never the tallest, fastest, or most highly recruited athlete at the Division I level, but he was certainly one of the hardest working competitors. He knew he was fighting genetic limitations as a 5'9" man with average-sized hands and feet, but he had instilled in him his father's "no excuses" mindset. He had the training background from his high school days in Sarasota to know how to use his skills to his advantage. If someone was going to beat him, they were going to have to work for it! If he was going to compete with guys who had a longer reach, then he was going to work on underwater kicking skills and flip turns at the walls to overcompensate for his shorter wingspan. "Working hard" was a concept Gregg could grasp, and when Coach Brewton saw that work ethic coupled with the best training background of any TCU swimmer, he started taking Gregg an hour away to Dallas two nights a week to swim with his much better club team to get extra training in. In the late '60s and early '70s, the TCU program would have considered a 5,000-yard workout a "big workout," whereas in Dallas, they were cranking out the yardage and at a much higher intensity. Gregg loved the competition and Coach Brewton loved doling out the extra yardage to him along with a select group of high school guys (and a few club swimming distance girls) who wanted it.

Gregg racing backstroke at TCU
Photo courtesy of Kathleen Troy

Just because the TCU team wasn't very good didn't mean they weren't still great teammates for each other. The group pulled together to work a little harder around Gregg. As the team captain, he managed to wrangle the guys every Wednesday afternoon for a little "team bonding." While some NCAA coaches might have their heads stuck deep in the ground like oversized ostriches when it comes to athletes drinking alcoholic beverages, as a coach, Troy always knew his collegiate athletes who were of the appropriate age let off some steam and got together around the local watering holes. He knew this because young Gregg and the Horned Frogs would push each other hard through Monday, Tuesday, and Wednesday practices to get to the Wednesday evening reward—$3 pitchers of beer and 25-cent hamburgers at The Frog Pond, the bar across the street from the pool. As a coach, in later years, Gregg will be the first to tell athletes and other coaches that drinking has no performance enhancing benefit that he knows of. He knows that drinks will negatively affect athletes' performance for days to come. But, in a private conversation, if you give him a minute to reflect and remember, he might tell you with a wry, small smile about the camaraderie and bonds that were formed at the Frog Pond and how those bonds helped him and his teammates not only power through three dollar pitchers, but also through 3000-yard kick sets in the water.

"Never let an education stand in the way of learning"

History had intrigued Gregg at TCU, which is what he majored in, but aside from teaching the subject, Gregg wasn't quite sure what he would do with a history degree. Walter Troy was bankrolling Gregg's education, as he would for Gregg's brothers and sisters. But Walter knew his son needed to be armed with knowledge and a degree that would always be pertinent. He wanted his son to be secure as he knew from his early years what it felt like to lack a profitable skill. Gregg's father pushed him to do all of his elective courses in education. While others were taking "Line Dancing for Beginners" and "Underwater Basket Weaving" for college credits, Gregg was learning about the positives and negatives of collective punishment in the classroom setting in classes titled things such as, "Classroom Management and Instruction." Since Walter was paying for school, Gregg had no choice but to grin and bear it.

Looking back, Coach Troy talks fondly of his education classes at TCU because coaching *is* teaching. Part of the requirements for obtaining one's teaching certificate is to serve as a student teacher in local schools. Acting as an apprentice for Henrietta Lehman, an experienced junior high and 9th grade teacher, in Fort Worth, Gregg learned, "your biggest weakness is that you're not very patient." Gregg, today, will laughingly concede that she was spot on with her analysis, and it took years for him to learn the patience that is required for optimal reception.

After Gregg's shadowing Ms. Lehman's class for just one day, she turned the class over to him and said, "The class is yours for the next three months. Here are the lesson plans, and here's where we are going; have at it."

Most coaches, trainers, and team assistants who have worked under Coach Troy in recent years are familiar with this type of delegation. Head Coach of the Sarasota Sharks, Brent Arckey, who was once a volunteer assistant at the University of Florida under Coach Troy, recalls a story regarding postgrads with a similar style of assignment:

I think Coach Troy is very good at taking calculated risks on certain people. There was a group of postgraduate swimmers, I think we were heading to a Grand Prix meet. I was in charge of taking redshirts and postgrads to Minnesota. He gave me all the info and told me to start doing some logistics on the trip and figure out what I was going to do, which required me to look at budget stuff and what it would cost. I remember picking up the phone to get a rental car, and I go through the entire deal and give them my credit card number and they say, "Well sir, you're not old enough to rent a car." I remember being as nervous as I could possibly be. I came back to him, nervous as hell, and tell him I'm too young to rent the car. I remember him looking at me, smiling, and saying, "Well, you'll figure it out." So, I had to trek postgrads who were older than me onto a train to the Metrodome, and we had to walk the rest of the way! I had Ryan Lochte and Steph Proud and others walking to their Grand Prix events. But he afforded me that opportunity to grow.

Ms. Lehman was instrumental in teaching Coach Troy the value of patience and the importance of knowing that each individual has unique capabilities (though some former swimmers of his will certainly chuckle at the idea of how effective that lesson was). She taught him to think up multiple ways to explain a concept or idea if your initial approach doesn't work. That individualized approach to drawing the best qualities from each athlete under his care would play a huge role in his success for years to come. There was nothing cookie cutter about any of Coach Troy's seasons, as each training block was comprised of different athletes at different periods of their lives experiencing different events and responding to coaching in different ways. Coach Troy's ability to adjust training plans based on the individual can be directly tied to Ms. Lehman's comments in Coach Troy's nascent teaching years.

Upon finishing TCU and at the behest of his father, Gregg applied to law school at the University of Texas at Austin. Gregg wasn't particularly fond of the idea of being a lawyer, nor was he outright against the idea. It just wasn't his passion. While waiting for the admission from UT, he returned home to Fort Myers to take up some part-time work for a few extra dollars. He took a middle school teaching job with the strict intention to only stay until January. Apparently though, his intentions weren't quite strict enough.

CHAPTER TWO

FORT MYERS

It's Just a Part-Time High School Job...Right?

Back in Fort Myers, Gregg jumped right back into the coaching saddle, assisting with summer league swimmers preparing for the Florida high school swimming season. It was something familiar to him, and something he was good at. There were two real high schools and teams in Fort Myers at the time. Fort Myers High, and the upstart, Cypress Lake, was on the south side of town. Fort Myers High was the established, elite, premiere place to be; Cypress Lake was the "school across town." Gregg was hired to help out at Cypress Lake after the basketball coach reached out to him to see if he would coach the swim team. With no swimming background, the basketball coach was happy to give Gregg the entire season's pay to just coach on deck. The basketball coach did all the paperwork and scheduling and never had to worry about missing basketball practice having Gregg on deck with the athletes. The only problem was Gregg was asked to take on the job in October, just months before he was slated to leave. Putting off law school for a year, Gregg took a middle school teaching job on the east side of town and threw himself into coaching the Cypress Lake high school team.

Aside from the on-deck coaching, and the teaching he was doing, the school had mandated one more aspect to his job that would have an enormous payoff in the long run. The school and athletic director *mandated* that Gregg attend the local swimming committee (LSC) meetings and the best of the yearly coaching clinics offered. Since beginning at Fort Myers, Gregg has attended each annual American Swimming Coaches Association's (ASCA) World Clinic. Attending yearly LSC meetings allowed Gregg to learn about local leadership issues, the planning of meets, the allocation of certain excess funds, and more. These LSC meetings gained him an insider's perspective on the decision-making process behind the swim meet development and implementation that he was affected by weekly. Similarly, while the information gleaned attending the ASCA World Clinics was typically of high quality, Coach Troy will tell you that the information, connections, and stories that help you most as a coach come from the taxi rides shared with other coaches or stories swapped over drinks at the hotel bar with colleagues at the end of the day. The foresight of the athletic director to empower his hire with knowledge with information from coaches Gregg respected was empowering. The athletic director's help in getting his new swimming coach to understand the power dynamics within his own sport was abnormal but appreciated. Few athletic directors are so wise and selfless. Gregg would repay that administrative assistance with the one thing that all athletic directors love—results.

Soon, Gregg was asked to take on the role of running the local Fort Myers club swim team, an offshoot of the Fort Myers High team. The club team only ran from June to October to prepare kids for the high school season and then generally disbanded until the following summer. There were only 60-90 swimmers on the team, but Gregg figured he could use the club team as summer employment for a few extra bucks before heading to law school. Gregg and Cypress Lake High would go on to beat Fort Myers that year in a dual meet, which had never been done. As it turned out, Gregg ended up having some exceptional athletes come out of the program. Paul Asmuth was one of the true workhorses to emerge from the Fort Myers program, along with David McCagg.

John was a pure distance swimmer who loved to "do more." As Coach Troy recalls, "He was a very directed athlete and a lot of fun to work with. He was dedicated to the sport. A coach's dream actually." His work with Coach Troy would inspire John to continue swimming for years to come. John would attend Auburn University and Arizona State University on his way to become one of the greatest professional marathon swimmers in history. He won the 23-mile "Around the Island Swim" in Atlantic City an unprecedented eight times with water temperatures ranging from the low '60s to the '80s. Among his other illustrious open water accolades are: three English

Channel crossings including the Men's record, the only person to complete the Nantucket to Cape Cod, Massachusetts, swim (31 miles), and the first person to circumnavigate Manhattan Island in under seven hours. Per Coach Troy, "His open water swimming set up the nucleus for today's open water swimming and helped open water become an Olympic event."

The Man Who "Made" Coach Troy: David McCagg

David McCagg went on to win U.S Junior Nationals that same year Cypress Lake beat Fort Myers. With the success and fun that came from fast swimming, a passion for the coaching profession was lit within Coach Troy.

David's story was unique. David was happy to train for Coach Troy and didn't mind getting up early for practice, at least he was as happy as teenage boys can be about getting up. The problem was he went to school across town and needed to get in the water 45 minutes to an hour earlier than anyone else on the club team to make it to school on time. While most swim coaches, even today, believe low morning practice attendance to be a reason to *not* hold morning practice, Coach Troy saw that one swimmer, with a similar work ethic to his own in his college days, as the exact reason why he *had* to get up earlier for one swimmer. He was determined to show the rest of his swimmers that by doing more and doing it better and by getting more repetitions in than your competition, you can improve. He found the right guinea pig to test his coaching beliefs in David.

David McCagg is Coach Troy's first great internationally successful swimmer. A seven-time gold medalist at the Pan Am Games and multi-time National teamer, world champion and world record holder, David was one of Coach Troy's earliest Fort Myers stars. The two lovingly share handshakes when they meet up, and David is quick to tell you, "I made Coach Troy as much as he made me!" His memories of those early years of training with Coach Troy are quite a trip...

Greg arrived in Fort Myers as head coach of FMSA at the age of 21. I think he was just six years older than me and fresh out of

TCU. *The whole team thought, 'Who is this nobody coming to coach us?' I especially thought that, as I was coming off my first Junior Nationals with a coach, Virginia (Ginny) Dunkle, who was an Olympic gold medalist.*

I was a cocky kid, the best on our team, and one of the best 14-year-olds in the country. Everyone told Troy his job would be easy, as I was such a great swimmer. Troy and I had a few run-ins, mostly because of my struggle for control. He knew he couldn't allow it and Troy usually won.

Troy gave me the foundation I needed to become the best in the world at what I did. He believed in me and wasn't going to let up on me. I learned very quickly that he cared, and he wanted me to be great.

Troy became my second dad. I shared everything with him, and I trained harder because of him, still with a bit of rebellion, though. At 16, I won Jr Nationals in the 100 free and in the 100 fly. I was second to John Ebuna in the 200 free, and second in the 100 back. All of those swims were national qualifying times for Nationals two weeks later. That was when I first realized it wasn't about me anymore, but about pleasing Troy. I needed a coach who wouldn't let me get away with anything and one who understood my inner makeup.

My junior year I won the high school state meet, and I was Troy's first State Champion, as well. When summer came around, I really didn't have anyone at my level to push me to the next level since I wanted to be the best in the world. I spoke with Eddie Reese, and he suggested I go to Jacksonville and train with Randy Reese. I was scared to death to leave Troy, as he was like my father and it felt the same as leaving my family. It was a very difficult decision, but I took with me a mindset and enough discipline to not only leave my senior year and everything I knew and loved, but to excel over the next eight years. It was all due to Troy and what he taught me.

To this day, I rely on his great tutelage and wisdom with my life; Troy has been instrumental in guiding me through everything.

Coach Troy worked in Fort Myers, as a teacher and swim coach, making $17,000 a year between the two jobs. Accounting for inflation over the course of several decades, that $17,000 would equate to roughly $76,000 today. The work between the two jobs, though, was never easy. Never the hypocrite, he worked as hard or harder than his swimmers did. Gregg would be up at 4:00 a.m. to make it to practice on time, off deck and in the car to get to work by 7:30 a.m. for his first period current events class (a senior elective, which often consisted of watching *The Today Show*), and in the classroom teaching until noon. Coaches will tell you that having an active presence at practices requires a high level of energy. Pacing the deck, observing strokes, teaching necessary adjustments, and motivating athletes to go harder, longer, and faster is draining physically, emotionally, and mentally. Teachers will tell you that planning lessons, maintaining order in the classroom, motivating children to find the joy in the subject matter being taught, and sustaining that energy for back to back to back classes is exhausting. Coach Troy brought an invigorating energy to both career pursuits. Neither job was easy, but it wasn't about doing what was easy. These jobs had become passions, and Gregg knew he had more to learn about each.

After a short lunch break, and with the approval of his athletically-minded principal, Coach Troy was allowed to leave school a couple of hours early to go watch Wes Nott and the Fort Myers High swim team practice. By learning and observing from the best in town, Coach Troy expanded and grew his "toolbox" of skills to use at practice. It was, and still is, unusual that Coach Nott allowed Coach Troy, the rival high school coach, to come observe his workouts. Most coaches are too egotistical and competitive to allow rival coaches an inside look at what's being done in practices. Similarly, on Coach Troy's part, it took an open mind and willingness to concede that someone else in town was coaching more effectively than he was. Few coaches are willing to admit they could benefit from observing how someone else does their job.

Coach Troy would then return to the Cypress pool and coach workouts until 9:00 p.m. before heading to the local pub for burgers and beers (if he had completed his grading and lesson plans that day). Gregg would stay out with friends if he had the time, always rising on time and with pep in his step the following day. His father's words would follow him, and Coach Troy's athletes, for years to come; *"if you're going to be a man at night, you've gotta be a man in the morning."*

CHAPTER THREE

THE BOLLES YEARS

Make the Move or Stay Put?

The small Fort Myers swimming community couldn't keep Coach Troy a secret for very long. His success was noticed by the big-name coaches across Florida. Hall of Fame Coach Jack Nelson and others in south Florida were impressed with the swimming coming out of Fort Myers. Terry Carlile at Jacksonville's Bolles School and the crosstown rivals at Episcopal under Randy Reese also caught wind of Coach Troy's success, even as they led winning seasons in north Florida.

After a few "down" years, where Bolles had finished as runner-up at the national level and runner-up at the highly contested state meet to Episcopal, Coach Troy was hired by Headmaster Harry deMontmollin Jr. to replace the coach who left to work with Jack Nelson in Fort Lauderdale. The team's numbers had depleted over recent years; there was no real club program, but Jacksonville was a promising place to live and the potential upside the school and boarding program offered were hard to pass up.

Another major draw to Bolles was the school's willingness to pay for Coach Troy to work for his master's degree while employed. While Gregg had since abandoned his father's wish for him of becoming a lawyer, the opportunity to work toward higher education while fulfilling his passion to coach seemed like an opportunity too great to overlook. Eventually, the potential the school offered and the true support from the administration would prove to be the difference makers in Gregg's decision.

Coach Troy had to consider the difference in salaries, though. The late '70s and early '80s, at least in coaching, saw far more coaches remaining in one area for an extended period of time to fully develop the talent of that town. Today, coaches have access to social media and the internet, which increases the information on potential available jobs and makes changing positions much easier. In the late '70s, Coach Troy had to consider the fact he'd already developed international level athletes in Fort Myers, it was an area he knew, and he had a relatively consistent work life. By taking the job at Bolles, he was essentially stepping into the unknown. He didn't know Jacksonville as well, and he would have an entirely new crop of athletes and support and wouldn't make nearly as much money! In hindsight, the move was a no-brainer. But, the most logical of minds in today's society would probably call the move a "risky one," at best.

Even though Coach Troy would make several thousands of dollars less each year at Bolles, compared to Fort Myers, his location in respect to the school/pool, the ease of living on campus as a dorm supervisor, the comparatively better training environment, and potential opportunities as a coach far outweighed the temporary dearth in funds. The acquisition of a master's degree in History Education from Jacksonville University also helped fulfill Gregg's unspoken and tacitly understood debt to his father. Walter's son might not have become a lawyer, but he was one of the most well educated and fastest rising coaches in America. Gregg remembers, "Sometime after my first couple of years, my father came out for the weekend and saw the campus and what we were doing. It was during that weekend that he came to realize the scope of what we were doing. After that, he was okay with my not being a lawyer; it was more about the mindset of, 'Whatever you're going to do, be great at it.'"

Coach Troy knew he could be honing in on the positive aspects of the new job and make his situation in Jacksonville one which everyone would envy. It would be challenging, he knew. There would be growing pains, there would be long nights sleeping at the dorms instead of his own house, but Gregg believed in the potential upside of Bolles and believed in his own abilities as a coach. He decided to take the job and make it an outstanding place to be.

Fostering Excellence

There are a few components required to foster high performance and excellence in any sport. While most nonathletes and administrators will name facilities, equipment, and ergogenic aids as the difference makers between good and great performances, coaches and athletes know the truth. The history of sport is brimming with examples of Olympians and world champions who have risen to greatness from squalor or dilapidated home environments. In the sport of swimming, two recent examples come in the form of Jenny Thompson and Ian Crocker. Jenny Thompson is one of the most decorated female swimmers in the world, while Ian Crocker is an Olympic gold medalist and world record holder. Both Jenny and Ian came from programs that trained out of five-lane, 25-yard pools, while others across the country were blessed with more pool space and premiere facilities. They did not come from teams with state-of-the-art facilities; they lacked certain equipment, and they had so few teammates that they lacked diversity and racing opportunities. Coaches and athletes both know the *only* things required for high performance are a strong relationship between coaches and their athletes and support from those around the coach and athlete.

When athletes trust their coach's knowledge and believe in the process described to them, coaches are able to push those athletes to new heights. Without that trust, it will never matter how much that coach knows about the intricacies of physiological training or development. As studies would show, decades later, coaches who were able to lead multiple athletes to Olympic gold medals, versus coaches who only helped one-time achievers, were different from their counterparts in that they were able to coach the group while still helping the individual. It is incumbent upon good coaches to find what each individual needs, and meet that need in the most positive way possible. As President Theodore Roosevelt is credited with saying, "People won't care how much you know if they don't know how much you care."

Keys to Getting Started

The Bolles School, from the early '80s to late '90s, would be on the hunt to steal the title of "*best boarding school in America*," knocking

Mercersburg Academy off the top. Wisely, the school understood what was necessary for high performance, and Coach Gregg Troy had an athletic director and headmaster who valued high performance above all else. When it came to swimming, the headmaster merely asked Coach Troy, "What do you need to succeed?" Coach Troy was able to take it from there. Without having to deal with bureaucratic tape and politics, the focus was on results and not outside distractions. Building relationships and trust between coaches and athletes was the first priority. Coaches were able to focus on acquiring the best information on technique, and guiding and disciplining swimmers who needed the framework, while avoiding time-sucking meetings with upset parents and the administration. The strong Bolles administration backed their coaches first and allowed them to do their job as promised.

Atypical of elite-level boarding schools and prep schools, the administration was able to remove Coach Troy's need to worry about raising money or collecting donations from alumni. The administration allowed the results from Coach Troy's coaching to draw in alumni, rather than relying on his charisma or networking skills. Bolles was, wisely, betting on the longevity of Coach Troy and his continued success to draw in donors in five, 10, and 15 years.

With the pressure of administrative duties largely lifted, Gregg sought to secure the title of "premiere high school swim team in America," and focused on what was required to send the largest possible delegation of high school students to the 1988, 1992, and the 1996 Olympic Games.

It was at Bolles that Gregg learned, as a coach it is vital to know what your administration considers to be your "goalposts." If administration cares about retention rates and you drive off athletes, you're in trouble. If the administration wants you to provide a fun and relaxed experience, but you're pushing for disciplined excellence, you're in trouble. If the administration won't even tell you what their goalposts are, the goalposts can be whatever they want, and you'll find yourself in hot water sooner rather than later. Gregg's connection with an understanding and intelligent administration was one of his first keys to success at Bolles.

Gregg began his time at Bolles by teaching full-time and watching over the boarding students in the dorms. Originally a military school for boys, Bolles was often the last resort for troubled young boys who were sent to the school's boarding program to be "whipped into shape." Coach Troy's value for discipline and structure, inherited from his father's lifestyle and Coach Brewton's Dallas workouts, was a major building block for the program in the initial years.

His first few years at Bolles were highlighted by a small, hard working group propelled by Suzane Crenshaw. Just as Paul Asmuth and David McCagg had been the workhorses and exemplary leaders in Fort Myers, Suzanne Crenshaw was the first true work-oriented athlete for Coach Troy in Jacksonville. Though only 14, and while she was never an elite, international star, Suzanne competed every single practice and drove her 17- and 18-year-old teammates crazy with her seemingly endless energy. Constantly touching their feet after catching up to the athletes in front of her and swimming over them viciously to make it back to the wall on increasingly quick intervals, Suzanne was quietly given an ignominious nickname (which has been omitted for her sake). Suzanne paid those girls no mind and kept on charging ahead. When she did try to take breaks, Coach Troy would quickly shuffle over to her lane and encourage and motivate her to go again, and to do it faster.

For years, it would be the workhorses who rose to the challenges thrown down by Coach Troy who would lead the teams he coached. Some coaches today will pinpoint Coach Troy as "just an IM coach" or "just a distance coach" or "just a *something* coach," but the truth is Coach Troy has been about *challenging the athlete* since his days at Fort Myers. As he says, "Those days were about how if someone's doing some, *more* is going to be even better." That type of attitude is generally shared by athletes who gravitate toward the longer events in swimming: the mile, the 500-yard freestyle, the 400-Individual Medley, or the 200-yard/meter events which require different pacing and more training. In later years, Coach Troy would be pigeonholed by naysayers and online trolls for not being a "sprint coach" or capable of producing speed. Interestingly though, in the mid '80s, Coach Troy was one of the first coaches to have four high school boys break the 3-minute barrier in the 400-freestyle relay. This meant each swimmer swam a sub- 45.00 second 100-yard freestyle; there are college programs today that don't have relays that fast! As he will tell you today, swimming fast isn't necessarily determined by "hard work," a term which he now actively dislikes using. To him, it's not about being "hard," and he believes the term has shifted what people believe it takes to be great. It's more about creating workouts that challenge athletes in the most appropriate ways to extend themselves beyond their last known comfort level. Some days a coach's job is getting an athlete just an inch beyond that last known comfortable point in order to ease them into doing something more difficult; other days coaching requires pushing an athlete further and challenging them *way* beyond their comfort zone.

It is difficult to define if the workhorses flourished because Coach Troy gave them the means to shine, or if average athletes became extraordinary because of the opportunities Coach Troy provided. Was it because they were motivated and driven by Gregg to succeed; or were those athletes already motivated and just needed the right person to help bring out their best? Likely, it is a confluence of both possibilities at once, and the potent combination was a vital component of Jacksonville's success in the '80s and '90s.

Early Bolles Years

When Gregg took the helm, the club team at Bolles was more than a cut above its high school team. The varsity team had just a handful of boarders and a few Bolles students, while the club team was comprised of swimmers from all over the Jacksonville area. Coach Troy's first meeting with the Bolles varsity girls team consisted of just five swimmers, one of whom had her arm in a sling...not exactly the ideal startup. The headmaster had warned Coach Troy at his interview, "The job isn't what you think it is." Coach Troy came to find out that warning meant almost all of the elite level swimmers and true athletes, like David Zubero and David Larson, had graduated and moved on. Eventually, the program would flourish on both sides, each side vying to outperform the other, but at the onset of Coach Troy's tenure, the club team had the upper hand.

Late fall afternoons at Bolles were a mishmash of whistles and coaches yelling. At one end of the pool, Coach Troy focused first on the varsity group, and then on the oldest swimmers in the club team's senior group. At the other end, a small, unaffiliated age group team was being run by Tom O'Hare. Tom, an outstanding coach in his own right, coached the Southside Sharks solely for young athletes to learn premiere stroke instruction. After just a few weeks of observation, Coach Troy took a leap of faith to convince Coach O'Hare that combining the two programs was in the best interest of both teams. By joining the well-taught Age Groupers on the Southside Sharks, with a larger senior team from Bolles, they created the Bolles Sharks, a team that better served the needs of the community from Learn to Swim lessons to senior level training.

The team would focus on swimming all of the strokes, not specializing in just one or two, while shamelessly overlooking the desires of overbearing parents. It is common for parents new to the sport of swimming to join a team and not understand the steps involved in the long-term development of their children. These parents often watch their 10-year-old son or daughter swim a short race like the 50 freestyle and absolutely dominate their competition. Every time their child races that event, they win by a body length or more. The parents then assume, "My child must be a 50 freestyler!" Knowledgeable coaches will understand that at 10 years old, some children are early bloomers who benefit strength-wise from earlier stages of puberty, while some children are later to develop and perform better once they have fully matured. At that age, a short race will always go to the more physically mature. Coach Troy made sure his coaching staff understood this basic tenant of swimming physiology and explained that training all strokes and racing a variety of distances would benefit the long-term development of the Bolles swimmers.

By running a team with a "swim all the strokes" philosophy, swimmers rarely become bored with workouts, remain fresh in training, experience muscular development from a variety of strokes, and tend to be better individual medley swimmers (races that combine all four racing strokes: butterfly, backstroke, breaststroke, and freestyle). As he'd always done, Coach Troy emphasized each athlete doing as much as they could *while still maintaining proper technique.* That concept would develop over time into a swimming reputation of surpassing all other teams in the second half of races and swimming better than anyone else in the hardest of events: the 200 yard/meter events of each stroke, the distance freestyle events, and the Individual Medley races. Beginning in the 1990s, internet trolls and uninformed coaches would brand Coach Troy's intense yardage as "garbage yardage" (even though there were certainly other coaches doing significantly more yardage at the time). They rarely knew, however, what actually went on behind the scenes and on deck at Coach Troy's practices. His ever-watchful eye was constantly checking for proper technique, and it was extremely rare for sloppy strokes to last longer than 50 yards before being caught and corrected.

Decades after the creation of the Bolles Sharks, K Anders Ericsson, a Florida State researcher, wrote the book, *The Road to Excellence: The Acquisition of Expert Performance in the Arts and Sciences, Sports and Games*, which would scientifically prove the point behind Coach Troy's insistence on proper technique and race quality repetitions. Ericsson used empirical data to suggest that a novice at nearly any task would require 10,000 hours of deliberate practice and purposeful attention to become a master at their task. Ten thousand hours averages out to about 10 years of practice. As Jeff Poppell, the current women's Head Coach at UF and once Head Age Group Coach for Coach Troy, said, "When it came to correcting one's technique, I always felt that Coach Troy had an inborn ability to hone in and identify the single one flaw, at that exact time, that he felt would make the largest impact on improving that individual athlete's performance. Details were extremely important to Coach Troy. What most coaches would view as trivial, he always seemed to see as particulars that made the difference in an athlete being good vs. great." At age seven, even the youngest Bolles Sharks swimmers were repeating as many correct repetitions as possible and their coaches honed in on deliberate practice for 10,000 hours, until they were masters by the time they were seniors in high school and preparing to enter the collegiate world of NCAA racing.

Tom O'Hare would be the first of four truly great Head Age Group coaches at Bolles who would guide the youngest athletes and newest coaches on the team toward greatness. He demanded excellence in technique that would become the foundation for the development of the program. Gregg firmly believed, and still believes, that groups for younger swimmers which focused on building upon skills and drills learned in prior groups would enable swimmers' careers with less injuries and more longevity. Over the course of the next eighteen years, Mal Henson, Rick Hattlestadt, and Jeff Poppell would all spend time teaching the strokes' fundamentals to children who would eventually be coached under some of the most rigorous training regiments executed in the United States at the time. That base of proper stroke development from the earliest of ages was a key reason that swimmers in the late '80s and early '90s were able to safely swim yardage that, by today's standards, would be considered extreme. With the application of near perfect stroke technique, an athlete has very few limits; the instant that technique is compromised, an athlete has *nothing but limits.*

Jeff Poppell was Coach Troy's last Head Age Group coach at Bolles. A University of Georgia swimmer, Jeff has a firm understanding of what it takes to swim at an elite level. His commitment to the sport mirrors that of his mentor, Gregg, and his path within the sport shares many similarities. After coaching as the Head Age Group coach beginning in 1993, Jeff served as the head coach for Bolles for several years before taking subsequent jobs at the University of Arkansas and Gulliver Preparatory in Miami, FL. At both schools, Jeff was able to charge the team cultures with pride and a dedication to raising each individual's potential. He would repeat as a Team State Champion in the 2A classification at Gulliver Prep for several years before taking a job as Troy's Associate Women's Head Coach at the University of Florida. Jeff was able to spend a few seasons learning from Coach Troy again before becoming the women's team's Head Coach in 2018. Here he speaks on the importance of Coach Troy's teaching and guidance:

As Head Age Group Coach at Bolles, under the direction of Coach Troy, I thoroughly enjoyed observing his senior practices to get a better understanding of the technical details that were being emphasized by him at that developmental level as well as the training rigors that were expected as a member of Coach Troy's senior national group. To me, that was invaluable in helping provide direction and focus in my role as age group coach to help facilitate the future success of our Bolles athletes when they entered the senior ranks of our club program.

International Success

Coach Troy's direct foray onto the international swimming scene came in part following the efforts of several Thai athletes enrolled at Bolles. In the late '80s, the Thai swimming federation selected several athletes who showed promise and potential to perform well at the 1992 Barcelona Olympic Games. The federation paid for them to attend school at Bolles. The Thai federation trusted that Coach Troy knew how to develop their promising athletes into superstars—a gamble they would later appreciate.

Ratapong Sirisanont, Niti "Bank" Intharapichai, and Praphalsai Minpraphal were fortunate enough to attend a respected American boarding school due to the generosity of their home country's federation, and they weren't about to squander that opportunity. Just as Suzanne Crenshaw drove practices with her intensity, the Thai athletes took to improving with a fervor. Coach Troy couldn't seem to give them enough! Set after set, week after week, training cycle after training cycle, the Thai swimmers seemed to feed off of the daily success and the idea of improving in the long course pool.

While the aerobic bases and endurance levels of the athletes grew, something else important was growing—the boarding program. When Coach Troy arrived at Bolles, the boarding program only accommodated about 35 students. After several years of success in the pool, though, the program expanded to host nearly 70 students— half of whom were a part of the swim team! The school administration then began to realize the cash cow that the swimming program could be. Thirty-five swimmers paying boarding school tuitions equaled influence and a small amount of power in Coach Troy's corner. Now was the time for Coach Troy to take his international experience a step farther.

With the blessing of the school's athletic department, Coach Troy accepted a role as the Thai international head coach for the several international meets leading up to the 1992 Olympic Games. Troy had coached international level swimmers before, but coaching such athletes as David involved turning over the swimmer to the international program's staff, and trusting they would thrive under the guidance of those coaches. Now, Gregg had an opportunity to be in charge. He would spend time overseas at the Southeast Asian Games and in board rooms observing and consulting on training cycles, travel plans, training stops and more. It was a learning experience, for sure. Coach Troy found that not every coach's wishes were met, athletes' needs were frequently cited but then overruled for monetary reasons, and certain deals were struck by administrators behind closed doors before board meetings were even convened. Nonetheless, his experience proved invaluable as he went on to coach with other international staffs, and it gave him confidence on deck at the 1992 Barcelona Games as the Thai Head Coach.

Peak Bolles Years

The Bolles football field was adjacent to the pool and it was pure, glistening heat. You could feel it from the pool deck. Every swimmer had just put in over seven thousand yards worth of work. While their body heat was radiating, the football field in Jacksonville, Florida, was baking in mid-October and only making matters hotter. The Bolles school early afternoon varsity practice was coming to a close. Student-athletes who attended Bolles were watched fastidiously by Coach Troy and Coach Larry Shoaf. Coach Shoaf, a bear of a man, had combined teams with Coach Troy several years ago. As the crosstown rival, the Episcopal club team had given Gregg a headache for several years. Now, by combining forces, the Bolles team was more competitive than ever. Like Caesar, combining the forces of surrounding enemies, Coach Troy created an empire. Troy was able to oversee the entire dominating program, while Larry, aside from his duties as an Assistant Athletic Director, was able to focus on the elite Senior National group.

Gregg, Larry Shoaf, and Martyn Wilby
Photo courtesy of Kathleen Troy

Even during warm down, the period of time where swimmers were swimming slower and purposefully recovering from their workout, excellence in technique and form was expected. There had been no deviation from technique expectations since the early days of Coach O'Hare's instruction. The swimmers climbed out gingerly and stood poolside, waiting for the final "see ya tomorrow, swimmers!"

Two swimmers, however, were not allowed the privilege of warm down just yet. The two girls were getting ready to battle it out in the 500 freestyle for the fourth and final position on the Florida High School Athletic Association State team roster. Bolles, like every Florida high school, was only allowed to take four athletes per event to the State series. Unlike every other high school in the state, Bolles had its pick of girls who could score in the top eight at the State meet. Most schools would be happy to have a single female break five minutes in the 500-yard freestyle, the longest event of the national high school order of events; Bolles already had three girls clocking in under four minutes and 55 seconds. The twenty-lap event requires endurance, speed, technique, a sense of pacing and certain drafting and racing skills. The opportunity to push athletes to new limits was not wasted on Coach Troy.

These two female swimmers dueling for the final spot on the Bolles State team were exceptional, make no mistake. Both girls were under automatic All-American time standards. One of the swimmers was a year and a half away from racing for a spot on the South Korean Olympic team in the 1996 Atlanta Games. Yet, one of the two would walk away without a spot on *the State team of the premiere boarding school in America*. The two girls were not the only ones who were challenged by this swim off. Never to be one to do things randomly, Coach Troy purposefully kept the team in the water to watch. He wanted the two athletes to feel the pressure and he wanted them to enjoy the feeling of *earning* a position on the team. By showcasing the swim-off, he could *show* the rest of the team and not just tell them what was expected as a Bolles athlete. As a Bolles swimmer, you might be one of the greatest athletes in your country and you may represent your country on the international stage, but that alone did not mean you had reached your ultimate potential and definitely did not guarantee you were living up to Bolles swimming's elevated standards. Such was the excellence demanded under the coaching of Gregg Troy.

The 20 years from 1977 to 1997 was chock full of talent on both the varsity and the Bolles Sharks teams. Coach Troy made school administrators and Bolles parents very happy with continuous State titles for both the male and female teams. Swimmers reveled in the yearly tradition of being crowned State Champions and jumping into the pool with their victorious coaches. Trophies littered the offices at the Bolles swimming offices, collecting dust. The annual scene created animosity among other high school and club coaches (as is wont to happen when one team is successful for stretches of time). But the murmurs and complaints against the boarding students specifically annoyed Coach Troy.

The comments crediting the boarding students for the collective team's success irked Coach Troy for one simple reason: Bolles swimming was great even without the boarding students! Proving a point to nobody but himself, each year Coach Troy would sit down on the Monday following the Florida high school state meet and go over the scoring sheets. In the years before computerized results, the process was time consuming and tedious. But Coach Troy would plant himself at his desk for hours, eliminate all the Bolles boarding students' points, and recalculate the results with nothing but Bolles' day school student athletes. The great years were when Bolles still won the State meet by 50 or more points without the boarding students' points; the *bad* years were when they only still won, but by 15 or less! Even with boarding student points removed, there was no question as to which was the top program in the state of Florida.

While the high school was busy winning State title after State title on both the men's and women's sides, the teams were also competing for "mythical National titles." High school Nationals don't exist, but a common practice among swimming enthusiasts is to compare the fastest results from each State meet at the end of each school year to determine who might win a theoretical National varsity meet. Though swimming seasons vary from state to state in the United States, the order of events and scoring are the same for all 50 states. For several years, under the guidance of Coach Troy, Bolles came out as the top program in the nation. The continued success of Coach Troy's leadership and teaching began to attract the attention of other schools and programs nationwide.

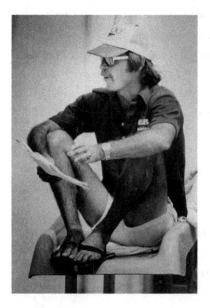

Lessons Learned: Mistakes Only a Head Coach Can Make

Though the wins were plentiful at Bolles, it wasn't all sunshine and rainbows and Pollyanna. Decades later, on deck in the O'Connell Center, Coach Troy used to frequently tell me, "Everyone wants to be Head Coach, but no one wants the problems that come with being Head Coach. Making

Gregg as head coach of the Bolles teams
Photo courtesy of Kathleen Troy

40

decisions is easy, it's dealing with the aftereffects that no one wants a part of."

Coach Troy will be honest with those who ask and will tell you that he struggles to understand some coaches' decision-making skills or planning because he was never anyone's assistant coach. From his days at Fort Myers to Bolles and eventually to the University of Florida, he was always the man making decisions regarding travel, nutrition, training, team dynamics, and racing decisions. Admittedly, he knows his history as a head coach is a major positive, but in ways it limits him. While at Bolles, he learned from two mistakes in particular that only a Head Coach can personally feel and be accountable for.

Tracing Results Back to the Source:

Early in the '80s, Coach Troy had a Bolles group that was not taking advantage of the two-and-half-hour sessions allotted to them. The swimmers were lethargic and just going through the motions of training without putting in major efforts or the necessary intensity to accomplish the goals they set. Coach Troy came up with a solution: he would limit workouts to only one hour. While most swimmers across the country might consider that a huge win ("Yay, less practice time!"), the Bolles swimmers recognized that suddenly they were going to be forced to do more, in less time, to still reach their goals. Coach Troy wanted to prove the point that they could still swim extremely fast at the end of the season by swimming at race speed for an entire hour each day. Once swimmers began to value the luxury of more practice time, he would return to two-hour sessions.

The plan went according to Gregg's predictions...until a certain point. The end of the short course (25 yards) season was unbelievable. The swimmers looked like they were flying across the surface of the pool. Underwaters were surreal, turns were tight; in short, it was a coach's dream. That dream quickly turned into a nightmare when the following long course (50 meters) summer began.

The lesson: A season's results are a combination of the work you did this season *and the work you did the season before*.

By short-changing the training volumes in the short course season, the swimmers were able to race well anaerobically for a season, but their bodies were unable to sustain the intensity in a longer pool with less walls to use as aides and masking agents. Swimmers are truly exposed in a long course pool; 50-meter racing shows which swimmers have done the appropriate amount of work and which swimmers have not. The Bolles swimmers suffered horribly that summer. Luckily, Gregg had amassed enough parent support and had the Athletic Director on his side. He was able to use the poor swims to explain to the team the value of consistency and hard work to "sell" them on returning to his tried and true methods.

Early in the 2010's, coaches became enamored with the "new-found" idea of Ultra Short Race Pace Training (USRPT). Young, green, high school coaches across the country loved the idea of training for only an hour a day and just doing short distances repeated at race pace speeds. Supremely educated and experienced coaches can tell you that in the 1950s, the positive and immediate improvement in performance in track athletes utilizing training nearly identical to USRPT were unable to sustain their performances which then drastically deteriorated. Coach Troy had personally learned in the '80s why USRPT couldn't be sustained in the long term development of athletes swimming events longer than 50-100 yards/meters. This knowledge had been painfully gained watching the sorry back halves of races in the summer following Bolles' one-hour, short course practices.

Where's the Line?

Overtraining in the sports world is defined as "a point where a person may have a decrease in performance and plateauing as a result of failure to consistently perform at a certain level or training load; a load which exceeds their recovery capacity. People who are overtrained cease making progress, and can even begin to lose strength and fitness."[1]

Examples of coaches pushing swimmers too hard over an extended period of time are rare in today's climate and coaching environments. Between the rise of helicopter parents, overbearing high school administrations, Gen Z athletes' dismal attention spans,

1 Walker, Brad. "Overtraining - Learn how to identify Overtraining Syndrome." *stretchcoach.com*. Retrieved 2016-05-17.

and collegiate restrictions on weekly training hours, there's a very small chance any athletes in today's world are sustaining such constantly high intensity training that they fall into the category of "overtrained." However, it's possible; and it was significantly more likely in the '80s era of "if some is good, more is better."

One of Coach Troy's training groups were once taken beyond the point of efficacy. Week after week of wear and tear on swimmers' shoulders and ankles and muscles had taken their toll. The yardage had piled up, the lactate hadn't been cleared properly, and swimmers' times in practice were suffering badly. It was only a few days after that "point of no return" that Coach Troy realized how hard the group had been pushed and for how long the group had sustained the efforts, but those few days were a few days too many. No one in the group seemed able to come out of their physical funk or the emotionally drained status they found themselves in. Heart rates remained elevated too long after workouts had already ended, and spirits were low even hours after practices had concluded. Their end of season performances suffered because of the overtraining and it would take weeks to get jump started back into fighting form.

The lesson: A Head Coach is in charge of the overall picture and ensuring the training is appropriate in its intensity, duration, and purpose at any given point in the season. Knowing where the line is for "too much" is vital. You won't ever know where that line *is*, though, if you don't take a person or group near or beyond that point. The lesson stuck with him for the rest of his coaching career. Many times, I personally saw him approach an athlete struggling through a workout after putting in eight, nine, or 10 days' worth of intense focus and effort. The swimmer was often given either a practice or two off, or an altered training schedule for the rest of the week. No one was ever exempted from work if they hadn't done the prescribed training beforehand, but very few were taken to that line of "too much" ever again.

Perhaps Caeleb Dressell can claim he saw the line, but that's for a later chapter...

Olympians at Bolles: A Stunning Resumé

Even at the premiere boarding school in America and coaching the mythical National high school champions, Coach Troy's ambition went unchecked and he aimed even higher. Similar to coaches Bill Belichick and Nick Saban, Coach Troy saw areas for improvement even when others only saw perfection.

The majority of coaches in America will never win a high school state title. Few will win one, never mind more than 15. Almost none will never lose a high school state meet and even fewer will win a mythical National title, never mind multiple. Yet, Coach Troy knew Bolles was capable of more and expected more from his athletes on a daily basis. Practices were breeding grounds for competition and from the competition grew unstoppable, machine-like athletes. The standard had risen to international and Olympic success. *Those* were the true markers of an elite swimmer under Coach Troy. That isn't to say Coach Troy couldn't appreciate the value of a fledgling high school swimmer passing the one-minute barrier for the first time in a 100-yard stroke event. But, with each passing year and each passing quadrennial between Olympic years, the swimmers (through their efforts) and the coaching staff (based on changes made to training) together raised the standard of what constituted "elite swimming."

While most swimming followers and online pundits will point to Coach Troy's international coaching resumé beginning with his time at the University of Florida and the Gator Swim Club professional group, Gregg himself will point to the Bolles' years as his most impressive group of Olympians and international swimmers for one simple reason—they were teenagers. In the two decades at Bolles, 13 of Coach Troy's athletes would go on to compete at the Olympic Games. Some of the biggest and most well-known names are:

Anthony Nesty

Anthony Nesty is one of the most prestigious swimmers, and eventual coaches, linked to Coach Troy. Nesty trained and competed in the country of Suriname throughout his teenage years. After competing in the 1984 Olympic Games in Los Angeles and placing 21st in the 100-meter butterfly, Nesty began training and attending school at Bolles. Known for his unparalleled work ethic and otherworldly butterfly sets, he was a training machine, and others were in awe of him. Nesty was known to do the same set designed for the distance freestylers, but he would do it butterfly! Under Coach Troy's training and mentorship, Anthony broke the prep school 100-yard butterfly record previously held by Pablo Morales. From there, Anthony would continue to achieve amazing results for the University of Florida as a repeat NCAA champion in the 100-yard butterfly (1990, 1991, 1992) and the 200-yard butterfly (1990). On the international scale, competing for Suriname, he won a gold medal at the 1988 Olympic Games in Seoul in the 100-meter butterfly, as well as gold medals at the 1990 Goodwill Games and the 1991 FINA World Championships.

The three time Olympian, National, Olympic, and World Champion would go on to become the Associate Head Coach for Men's Swimming at the University of Florida, coaching alongside Troy, before taking the helm as the Men's Head Coach for the University of Florida in 2018.

David and Martin Zubero

David returned from his freshman year at the University of Florida to train under Coach Troy in preparation for the 1980 Olympic Games in Moscow, where he won a bronze medal in the 200-meter backstroke for Spain. While the University of Florida coaching staff, including Head Coach Randy Reese, certainly helped prepare him well, David returned to Bolles for a familiar training site and a coach he knew could help guide him. David's success would encourage his younger brother, Martin Zubero, who would win the gold medal in the 200-meter backstroke in the 1992 Olympic Games in Barcelona.

Greg Burgess

Overlapping with Martin Zubero, Greg Burgess joined the Bolles School after his father, a U.S. Army serviceman, was transferred to a Jacksonville base. Greg was used to purposeful training with great coaches, as he'd come from the North Baltimore Aquatic Club (NBAC) in Maryland. The renowned swim club is known today as Michael Phelps' original swim club. At Bolles, Greg trained with some of the toughest athletes in the sport at the time in preparation for the 1992 and, eventually, the 1996 Olympic Games. "I walked in my freshman year, and he basically told me to get in a lane with Anthony Nesty and follow him," Coach Burgess recalls. "It was tough. He was tough. It was his way or the highway, and we all knew that, but he sure knew what he was doing."

Developing character and a disciplined mindset was not something that coaches could bestow upon swimmers by being nice and kind. Coach Troy and the Bolles staff did their best to breed a champion's mindset for athletes like Greg Burgess through discipline and structure.

The work paid off, though, as Greg would go on to compete at the University of Florida. While at UF, he would win the 200-yard Individual Medley and 400-yard Individual Medley at the 1993 and 1994 NCAA Championships as well as set four American records: two in the 200 IM and two in the 400 IM He received 12 All-American honors and earned spots on both the 1992 and 1996 U.S. Olympic teams. He would take home silver, finishing second in 1992 and sixth in 1996.

While Coach Troy will only claim Greg's success during his high school years, the effect his coaching had is undeniable. "You were always nervous when he'd light into you and start to walk away. It's like he would get a few steps away and then remember something else you did wrong and come skipping back to let you know...loudly. You remembered what you did wrong for a long time." Greg Burgess is currently a coach in north Florida for a club team and "tries to emulate everything he ever did. Every part of my practices come from what we did in high school. We're IM based, we swim a bit of everything, and we work hard."

In 1997, Greg Burgess joined the U.S. Marine Corps (he would later be promoted to Major) and is one of just a few American Olympians to ever volunteer for military service following their athletic career.

Trina Jackson:

A wildly competitive athlete, Trina Jackson attended school and trained at Bolles from 1991 until 1995. At the Pan American Games, in 1995, Trina would win the 800-meter freestyle with a time of 8:35.42, ahead of the then Olympic champion, Brooke Bennett. Her success at the international level helped Trina win the 1995 Swimming World Magazine High School Swimmer of the Year.

The years of preparation under Coach Troy at Bolles paid off at the 1996 Olympic Games in Atlanta, where Trina won a gold medal on the 4 x 200-meter freestyle relay for the USA. She was also a silver medalist at the World Swimming Championships. In her four years as an Arizona Wildcat, Trina was a 15-time All-American qualifier. She took home the NCAA title in the 1650-yard freestyle in both 1997 and 1998, and she was also a member of the NCAA Championship 800 freestyle relay team in both 1998 and 2000.

CHAPTER FOUR

THE EARLY YEARS WITH THE UF WOMEN

Evaluate and Decide

Following the '96 Games, Coach Troy did what he always did at the end of a season—he evaluated the performance of his team and of himself as a coach. Gregg was thrilled with many performances from the summer, but knew something was amiss. Coaching at Bolles had begun to feel stale. There was a bit of an uneven playing field in Coach Troy's mind, and he craved a new challenge. Coach Troy had also grown frustrated with the number of athletes who left the Bolles swimming program and failed to develop at the collegiate level as he had anticipated and hoped they would. It was frustrating as a club coach to hand off elite level swimmers to college coaches who couldn't help those athletes take the next step.

Swimming was beginning to shift; older athletes were performing better and were receiving better help in most instances. If Coach Troy wanted to shift with the sport and coach athletes who were more physically and mentally mature, he would have to make a change.

Gregg's wife, Kathleen, enjoyed Jacksonville since her family had roots in the area. Gregg's oldest son was about to start high school; Gregg knew that if he wanted to make a coaching change, it would need to be to a program nearby and it would need to be now or never. Coach believed in a phrase he'd been told before, "You never want to leave when your program is down. Leave when it's better than how you found it." Coach Troy would leave his job as head coach. The job position that would remain the *signature, pinnacle job opportunity in club or private school swimming in the country for decades*. It should not be understated how significant a jump the program made from the late '70s to the late '90s. Many talented and capable coaches would follow Gregg as head coach of the Bolles program, but the sense of tradition and expectations of elite state, national, and international representation was born from the Troy era.

By 1997, Bolles was at a high point; the Florida Gators and Athletic Director, Jeremy Foley, couldn't have called at a better time.

Arriving in Gainesville

Gainesville is a small college town in northern Florida, roughly an hour and a half southwest of Jacksonville and about two hours north of Orlando. Swamplands and forests make up the landscape, and heat, humidity, and summer rains are notorious in the city. Throughout campus, the Spanish moss hangs from pine trees that line the roads and the edge of Lake Alice. The midsummer humidity is thick enough that you feel like you can reach out and run your fingers through it. But, cotton candy-colored sunsets, the crickets and cicada bugs chirping at dusk, and the serenity of nature throughout campus are just some of the marvels of being in Gainesville.

The town is fiercely loyal to the Gators' college teams, and athletics are a uniting force of the town. Regardless of the sport, home games, matches, meets, and events are always big time events. Home events are frequently sold out and bleachers are packed to capacity. Orange and blue t-shirts and apparel are seen around every corner, on campus and off. Gator football game days are a circus unto themselves. Fans from across the state and throughout the city wake up before the sun to migrate to campus grounds for tailgating and carousing before beelining to Ben Hill Griffin Stadium to watch the kickoff. The heat and humidity are oppressive for opposing teams, which earned the venue the apt nickname, "The Swamp."

Coach Troy had been offered a position at the University of Florida several years before he actually accepted the position. At the time of his original offers, he didn't believe the change of environment was right for him or any better than what he had built at Bolles. Perhaps the truth of the matter is the position just wasn't quite challenging enough to warrant his attention yet. The Gators had finally secured the man they wanted leading their swimming program.

Stephen C. O'Connell Center Natatorium
Photo Courtesy of the University Athletic Association

But by 1997, the Gator's women's team, which had won SECs for 10 straight years, had slipped at the conference level to the middle of the pack. The challenge of bringing the Gators out from the middle was a tough task even for the ultimate task-oriented coach. Rising from the middle of the pack to the top was even harder than rising from the bottom to the top. Being in the middle meant that the Gators were good, but something spectacular was required to beat the best. Gregg believed he was up for that challenge.

To his fortune, Gregg had the support of a one-of-a-kind administrator. UF Athletic Director Jeremy Foley was, according to Coach Troy, "a visionary. He was at the cutting edge and understood high performance for almost every sport. He really understood what coaches went through on a day-to-day basis and supported us." Just as he had been in Fort Myers and at Bolles, Gregg was once again backed by an athletic director who didn't stand in the way of his professional coaches. Mr. Foley and Gregg had intimate and frank discussions about Gregg's vision for the future of Florida swimming. Gregg told Mr. Foley that he "didn't want to go about building the program the traditional way." Coach didn't want to have to "sell his soul for a 17- or 18-year-old to win some relays for a National title." Building the program around people interested in being their absolute best (which took many to the international stage) meant Coach Troy could build a different, bigger, and better program.

Pitching the idea of "international success prioritizing NCAA success," was a risky tactic, and remains so to this day, but Jeremy Foley recalls, "It wasn't a problem at all to me. At Florida, we had a history of international success even before Coach Troy. Coach Reese and Skip Foster had elevated the programs to that level. I was fine with him trying to foster both, and we wanted to offer that too. The other thing to remember is, the Olympic success that Gregg had only enhanced the overall brand for the Florida Gators. We loved that!"

Gregg had a game plan. College coaching would be different from club coaching. Some coaches are mistaken about the time required, both to be a club coach and also to be a college coach. College coaches typically spend a great deal of time doing "dry side" activities: paperwork, recruiting, and planning logistics. Many complain about the lack of "wet side" coaching they actually get to do on a daily basis. Club coaches share some of those dry side duties (minus the recruiting), in addition to dealing with parents on a daily basis, taking calls, and frequently sitting in on meetings. That's not to say college coaches don't deal with parents, they do; they just usually have one enormous meeting at the end of the season at which *everything* is rehashed at once. Gregg was in for an interesting adjustment, to say the least.

The history of sports is littered with examples of coaches who have elevated from collegiate level of coaching to the professional leagues and floundered. Nick Saban's stint as the Miami Dolphins head coach is just one example. After success leading LSU to a College National Football title, he thought he could make it in the professional league. But after fruitless seasons with the Dolphins, he returned to the NCAA system and the Alabama Crimson Tide and settled into his historic head coaching role. Not every story is one of failure, however; there are many coaches who climb the ladder and succeed, like Pete Carroll and Jimmy Johnson, two seemingly natural leaders. The jump from being a top-level high school and club coach for the past 20-odd years to being an NCAA head coach for the first time was something akin to making the jump to the NFL.

Gregg was ready to adjust to the life of a college coach. He was encouraged by the incredible support the university was capable of offering and was keen on having a much smaller group of swimmers to focus on. Using his administrative experience with the boarding program at Bolles, Gregg was able to mentally adjust to the dry side of collegiate coaching quickly. In the past, he was worrying about over 300 athletes in the Bolles club program, in addition to the varsity teams, parent booster boards, and an entire aquatic program. Now Coach Troy would be able to focus solely on the 30 women composing the team and the recruits he hoped to draw in.

After coach Randy Reese, Chris Martin had served as the head coach from 1993-1996, before handing over the program to Kevin Thornton for just two years (1996-1998). The turnover in the years after Coach Randy Reese had affected the culture of the team. With no truly unifying figure at the head of the team, the women were without direction. Coach Troy came to Gainesville acting as a sieve. He knew he would need to filter the quality information the outgoing coaches offered while relying on his own intuition and years of experience.

Remembering his first years at UF, Coach Troy recalls, "I was always pretty close with Skip Foster, one of the former UF Swimming coaches who was still in town, and we communicated regularly about the team. He gave me pretty good information, which I trusted as I started out with those girls. We knew they would be special if they could all get on the same page. From day one, I told them, 'You're either on the bus or off the bus; but either way, I'm driving.'"

Game Plan

In the swimming world, the typical game plan of incoming NCAA head coaches is to coach and recruit sprinters. By coaching and recruiting sprinters, most coaches aim to do well in short races and relays where points are worth double. Coach Troy looked at the team he inherited and recognized the low-hanging fruit; there were points to win in all the events other coaches were ignoring. Instead of focusing on sprints, Coach Troy took to recruiting and coaching women who performed well in mid- to long-distance events such as the 200-yard events, the 400-yard individual medley, the 500-yard freestyle, and the mile. These swimmers appreciated the well-deserved attention, and Coach Troy enjoyed developing them with his signature gruff methods.

Not every athlete took to Coach Troy's grinding training plan. Donna S*, as Coach Troy describes, was by far the best swimmer in the group when Coach took over. She had the skills to perform under pressure at the conference and national levels, but she wanted her own individually detailed training program. Coach Troy and his top assistant from Bolles, Coach Wilby, knew that the program couldn't be built around that "individual-first" style. Coaches would need to dictate the programming, establish the cultural standards, and set the tone. Coach Troy and Donna S* had several conversations, which ultimately resulted in her departure from the team. She would be better suited at a program where her individual needs could be prioritized over the needs of the collective group.

"When it comes to culture, you have to understand that it is constantly changing. Culture is not self-perpetuating, especially at the collegiate level. One quarter of your team is outbound and another quarter is incoming. Those incoming freshmen are arriving from all over the country and, in some cases, the world. They are all coming in with different memories, different standards, and from different cultures themselves. So, culture isn't something that is just set on week one and something you can talk about in a meeting every six weeks. You're constantly shaping your team's culture," Troy notes. Though it was difficult to part with one of the best athletes in the group, the women benefited from the overall cohesion and focus that came that first year. They had underachieved for a few years, and knew it, so with a little work and correlating results, the swimmers knew they were on the right path.

"It's really too bad that Donna S* and I crossed paths at that point in my career," says Coach Troy, "because she was a fantastic person and incredible athlete. It wasn't anything personal, it was just what the group needed at that point. And it's really too bad because if she'd been my athlete in 2019 with the professional group I have now, she'd fit right in! Individualistic programming isn't a bad thing; it just needs to be implemented and supported based on the group you have as a coach."

CHAPTER FIVE

COMBINING THE GATOR MEN AND WOMEN

Melding Two Into One

Just one year after signing on as the UF Women's Swimming head coach, the men's and women's teams joined forces uniting as a single team under Gregg Troy's tutelage. After thoughtful consideration, Athletic Director Jeremy Foley believed that combining the two Florida swimming programs was the best route to take.

"I'm just calling it like it is. Sometimes in this job, trying to go find the 'next great coach,' you find that the pool of applicants is sometimes shallow. At that time, great coaches wanted to stay where they were at. So, I turned to Gregg and asked his thoughts on the situation. He'd done it before; he'd run a successful combined program at Bolles, and I was confident he could do it with us. He just really *wanted to do it,* and he had a plan. He laid out his vision for me and it was a style that I was sold on," recalls Mr. Foley. "He was *direct,* and we were looking for a winner."

Taking over for legendary Ron "Styx" Ballatore, Gregg found himself in charge of two different halves of one larger whole. Styx had been the quintessential "guy's guy" and had coached the Gator men as *men.* Profanity was allowed and used frequently; motivation was harsh and pointed, but Styx was able to pull the best from men and they loved him for it. The Gator men were extremely good "racers" and loved to go eyeball to eyeball as often as possible, but there was something lacking in their ability to train. They lacked certain gritty tendencies. Coach Troy noted it mentally and would soon have a chance to help build the gumption they lacked.

The men had been in the middle of the pack at the Southeastern Conference (SEC) race at championship season, but each year saw improvement in their standings at the NCAA Championships. Placing near the top 10, or just inside, the Gators could perform when it counted at the national level. Coach Troy saw the potential and knew he was just a few pieces away from making the Gators men's swim team a perennial top 10 powerhouse. With *exactly* the right pieces, they might even crack the top three in a few years.

Since the men and women had trained around each other for several years and even practiced together during the summer months, the joining of the programs was fairly seamless. What helped the two teams was that they fraternized both in and out of the pool. The Florida swimmers were always known to party hard, but never harder than they worked. The women were already accustomed to Coach Troy's ways and most had bought into his vision for the future. They were able to encourage the men, already great racers, to trust Troy's training process.

As opposed to other collegiate conferences that run two separate meets, the SEC Championship meet runs men and women together during the same week and at the same site, meaning a natural fit for joint training and preparation. The team's goals could be directed to men and women at their mixed practices, and athletes were familiar with their peers' individual goals. The closeness of the group allowed everyone to push and encourage each other daily in the water, instead of having to wait to catch up before or after practice. Strong women raced hard in practice and gave slower men the impetus to perform better. Men struggling to break through to the elite level had powerful men and women to race at every practice, and strong women had elite level men to push them past their most fatigued points. Women aiming to perform at the pinnacle of their sport were able to turn to elite Gator men and were never denied an all-out effort on par with, or faster than, anything they would encounter in any SEC or NCAA final heat.

To complete his understanding of the freshly combined program, Coach Troy wisely sought the advice of a fellow Gator Coach, Donnie Craine. Donnie was the UF Head Diving Coach, but he also knew the sport of swimming. A Florida native who grew up around the water, "he understood the sport and could give me really good feedback about the team. He could give me insight about high quality athletics, but because he wasn't 'a swimming coach,' his opinions were refreshingly neutral and unbiased." He was a fantastic sounding board for Coach Troy for years to come. Under Coach Troy and the Gator staff's guidance, the UF men's and women's swim teams were trending in the right direction.

Blue Collared Recruits

The Gator coaching staff under Gregg Troy, now made up of Coach Martyn Wilby, Coach Anthony Nesty, Coach Bryan Shrader, and Volunteer Assistant Buddy Baark, took a different approach to recruiting those first few years. Yes, recruiting distance-based athletes was odd already, but the Gator staff added another wrinkle. Instead of chasing after "5-star" recruits, the Gators used their club team coaching connections, talking extensively with Florida club coaches to find diamonds in the rough.

Bryan Shrader was Coach Troy's first sprint coach, brought in from USA Swimming, and a man with great connections in the state of Florida. The coaching staff talked with club coaches constantly, finding athletes they believed were on the cusp of doing something special. They ended up recruiting a good number of athletes who were willing to outwork anyone, swim any event asked of them, and willing to generally *do more.* The combination of exceedingly tough, blue-collared, work-oriented athletes who were competing daily on a unified team, and the results they saw at the end of season, was electric. Hard-nosed, late bloomers found their place at the University of Florida.

The Gator coaches knew they could take hardworking and driven 3- and 4-star recruits, and coach them into scoring NCAA athletes. This avenue would be more difficult and would require more effort than coaching athletes who were already superstars, but just because it would be tough wouldn't be a reason to shy away from it. The Gator coaching staff took it upon themselves to find the local Florida boys who needed a landing pad and high-quality coaching. Some of the boys the UF staff received commitments from had been passed over by other teams, and this created a chip on their shoulders. Troy would exploit those chips in the future. Proving to future recruits, through these success stories, that they would develop and improve at Florida, became an in-house point of pride.

"Martyn Wilby was someone I brought over from Bolles because he was an excellent coach in his own right and definitely one of the greatest assistant coaches ever. Assistant coaches are really there to pick up the juggling balls that head coaches drop, but Martyn was so good at what he did that he could anticipate the balls I'd drop and catch them before they hit the ground," recalls Troy. Coach Wilby is also fortunate to have the gift of gab. The man can talk to anyone, about anything, and have them in stitches by conversation's end. These are precisely the qualities you want in the man that is out on the road recruiting. Wilby's ability to charm every recruit's mother on the eastern seaboard, while sharing a pint with the recruit's father, and simultaneously capturing the attention of the prospective recruit, himself/herself was a skill to behold. (To any NCAA officials reading this, that's called hyperbole. Coach Wilby would never enjoy a frosty pint whilst recruiting, so chill.)

Coach Martyn Wilby
Photos Courtesy of the University Athletic Association

Athletes Who "Buy In"

One thing new or inexperienced coaches don't understand is, aside from being a teacher, mentor, and a guide for athletes, coaches are also salesmen and saleswomen. We are *always* selling our programs. Coaches are salespeople, plain and simple. When new, prospective parents walk on deck and ask why they should select your club as the place for their child, that is an opportunity to use your salesmanship skills! Recruiting is also selling your program on the idea that your city and university is the next place a potential recruit should call "home." Athletes who accept the philosophy of a coach, trust that a coach's process can yield results, and believe in the methods used to execute the philosophy and process, are athletes who have "bought in." Without buy-in, coaches have an extremely difficult time getting athletes to achieve their desired goals. Without buy-in, coaches can feel like they are communicating with a brick wall.

Coach Troy's training plans, and the effort the Gators put into following these plans, produced great results the first few years of the joint program. But, Coach Troy learned an extremely valuable lesson on the value of athlete buy-in from his experience with Florida junior, Alec Moreno*. Coach Troy's treatment of Alec would have lasting effects decades into the future.

Alec had been recruited by Coach Styx Ballatore and knew Coach Troy from their combined summer training months. Alec and Coach Troy had talked several times over those months about how great he could potentially be, but it wasn't until Alec's senior year that Coach Troy was directly responsible for this young man's swimming.

According to Coach Troy, "Alec was as close to Ryan Lochte as an athlete can be, and this was years before Ryan was on the scene. Alec was dynamic. He was a hell of a racer, he was a personality, and he got the other guys going. He had really strong leadership qualities, and he was a bit of a loose cannon—kind of wild. He was just a lot of fun to be around. But he wasn't very consistent with practices, and he didn't take training very seriously." That inconsistency in training wasn't going to work with the culture Troy knew was necessary for success.

"We had to have a few talks over the course of his fall semester in his senior year. It wasn't hashed out in a single meeting. We had to really talk about it, and I had to work hard to convince him to do it my way. He had to quit drinking so much, he had to buckle down, and he had to be consistent." Alec, as Coach Troy would put it, had to "get on the bus." And he did.

Alec proceeded to knock out week after week of incredible training and became more consistent than ever before. The weeks turned into months, and pretty soon, Alec was competing at the SEC Championships. Even without shaving, he qualified for the NCAA Championships in the 200-meter backstroke. Since that was an Olympic year, the NCAAs were run in a 25-meter course, which was radically different than what any program was prepared for. Even so, Alec wasn't concerned and would go on to win the 200-meter backstroke!

Coach Troy was thrilled about Alec's success and returned to Gainesville with his mind reeling. Coach believed Alec stood a chance to make the U.S. Olympic team based on the time he'd gone at NCAAs and went to work hashing out a long-term training plan for him. A week passed and Coach Troy had his plans ready, when in walked Alec fully dressed.

Before Coach Troy could finish his first sentence about Olympic plans, Alec smiled and said, "Coach, I did even more than I thought I could do. You pushed me to an NCAA title. I never had any intention of going out for the Olympic team; I'm content with what I've achieved." Just like that, Alec was done.

Decades later, Coach Troy would bump into Alec and his wife at a Florida football game and laugh and shake hands as friends. "It was disappointing to me as a coach, for sure. I wasn't ever disappointed *in* or *with* him, just disappointed at the circumstances and what could have been. But, seeing him and how happy he was, it was an amiable situation, and I understood how he felt. What he did was really special for him, it was special for the university, and it was special to me as a coach." It took an athlete of Alec's caliber to teach Coach Troy a lesson he would use repeatedly with his college athletes over the next several decades: **if they buy-in, they will be capable of really amazing things. If they decide that they don't want to do it, though, you shouldn't worry yourself. They aren't going to get over that mentally.** "The situation with Alec helped clarify for me that coaches are also mentors. You have to be aware of who wants to be helped and who wants to be pushed."

Since Gregg's own sons were just becoming athletes themselves, the lesson at the pool transferred over to his family life. Gregg brought home the example Alec set of "finishing something you start," and Gregg made sure his own sons really understood the value in that. Gregg saw his sons develop as people and athletes as they ran track through high school and college but wouldn't fully appreciate their understanding and grasp of the lessons until later in life.

CHAPTER SIX

RYAN LOCHTE EMERGES

Recruiting: Jeah!

Years before his shiny silver hair and gold grills donned the Olympic podium, years before reality TV cameras followed him around, and years before one of the greatest University of Florida Gator athletes found repeated Olympic glory, Ryan Lochte had more in common with average teenagers than he didn't. An avid skateboarding and surfing fiend from Daytona Beach, he was equally as likely to be at the beach or basketball courts as he was likely to be in the training pool. Ryan looked the part of a beach bum, with a tanned 6'1" broad-shouldered frame topped with long shaggy hair.

In the swimming pool, Ryan was exceptional, especially compared to the rest of the state of Florida's high school swimming population. Coached by his father, Steve Lochte, Ryan was a repeat individual state champion in the 200-yard Freestyle and 500-yard Freestyle and was the best of the state in his junior and senior years by a wide margin.

As Coach Troy remembers, "He had unbelievable racing skills as an Age Grouper and stellar technique." But even as he developed into a talented senior swimmer, he was by no means exceptional on a national or world level, yet... Times of 1:38 and 4:25 in the 200-yard and 500-yard freestyles, respectively, were strong swims for the high school senior, but Ryan would need something more to put him over the edge into the company of the elite.

Following his senior year of high school swimming, with college on the horizon and the 2002 U.S. National meet approaching, Ryan was motivated to bump up his concentration in the water. This newfound intensity would result in his winning the top award for the state of Florida, the "Florida Dairy Mr. Swimming" award.

When it came time to decide on college, Ryan had his choice of schools. Among the schools vying for his college commitment included: Texas, Auburn, Michigan, and Southern California, along with Gregg and the Gators. None of the other schools pushed for Ryan particularly hard, though. Coaches watched his results at a variety of competitions and noticed there were some irregularities when he competed outside of the state of Florida. Ryan's results were a little off at major meets outside of his comfort zone, and he was labeled by some as "flaky." Most schools came to Ryan with offers of a 25 percent scholarship or less. Coach Troy figured he had the easier sell compared to other schools. Gainesville is still within the state so in-state tuition would be a benefit, and Gainesville was close enough to home to go back if Ryan ever got homesick. But it was also far enough away that he would be without parental supervision in a new city that felt different than his hometown, Daytona Beach.

Coach Troy trusted Steve Lochte's abilities as a coach. He knew Steve was one of the best at training swimmers hard, but not overtraining them. Coach Lochte was adept at challenging his swimmers to race, and Troy believed him when he said that Ryan was capable of being excellent on the world stage. Ryan fit the bill for Florida's recruiting standard: hard-nosed, diamond in the rough who just needed a little polishing. With his trust in the Lochte father-son duo, Troy offered Ryan a full scholarship to UF and outlined a path that would lead him onto the U.S. Olympic team.

"You have to plant the seed in the minds of those who are capable. If you're afraid as a coach to plant seeds of potential greatness, they won't get there. If you plant too shallow of a seed and it's too easily achieved, they won't aim for more. You have to trust that those with superior mindsets can handle the idea of *true greatness*," according to Troy.

Other schools were talking to him about how he would add to a team vying for an NCAA title, while trying to draw him in with no financial assistance whatsoever. For Ryan, the difference between coaches and the offers they presented him was like night and day. The Olympic team? That resonated with the Lochte family.

As Ryan recalls, "Even being ranked top 10 in the nation in the 200 and 500 free didn't get me on many people's radar. But Coach Troy had a few guys back out of committing to school at the last minute, so he showed up in my living room one evening. He told me he had a full ride for me if I wanted it and I was just laughingly like, '**** yeah, get me outta here!' Then he started talking about plans for the Olympics. Having him talk about me getting to the Olympic level was a weird moment for me. It was like, 'Is this guy smoking crack? How can he think I'm Olympic caliber?' So, immediately, right there, I knew I had a guy who believed in me."

There was one more poignant moment Ryan remembers fondly. What *truly* sold Ryan on the University of Florida program, and Coach Troy in particular, was when Troy said, "I'm going to treat you like my own son."

"That was such a big thing for me," remembers Ryan. "Family means so much to me and hearing him say he was going to take care of me like one of his own, I knew automatically that that was what I wanted."

Before checking into his dorm in Gainesville in the fall, Ryan would score the most points at U.S. Nationals and was crowned the individual high point winner at the U.S. Open in Minneapolis. Little did Ryan know, though, the accolades and success were just beginning.

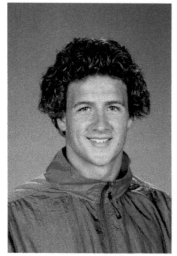 

Photos Courtesy of the University Athletic Association

The Differences in Training: Ryan Lochte vs. Everyone Else

While Lochte was by no means unsuccessful his freshman year, it took him about 18 months in the new training environment to get used to Troy's formula. Early on, Ryan was able to produce fast swimming in practice, but linking *multiple* great practices together was tough. It took many months of deliberation and meetings between coach and athlete before Ryan began to really grasp the concept that *consistency of effort* was what had been missing.

"Troy yelled at me pretty regularly, just rarely *at* swim practice. I never got special treatment, which I think is amazing. He treated me like everyone else. I really only heard from him when I screwed up outside of the pool, which is totally understandable," Ryan reminisces.

Central to performing well on bigger and more intense stages was gaining confidence and Troy knew that the place to gain confidence in one's ability to perform was in the training pool. He also knew that a swimmer's confidence didn't grow overnight, it came from weeks of completing vigorous, high-quality practices, gaining knowledge in the pool, and really believing that one was capable of doing hard tasks. One practice after the next, Ryan's sea legs grew a little sturdier, and with consecutive weeks under his belt and an entire training block accomplished, Ryan had built up the confidence he needed to race like never before. A newly self-assured Lochte would begin to thrive under the calculated guidance of Gregg Troy.

The Only Act of Rebellion

"There was only one true instance of rebellion from Ryan in the first 10 years I coached him," recalls Troy. "Somewhere midseason of his sophomore year, we had a malcontent group of underachievers on the team. They weren't performing really well in training and were complaining about practices being too tough and whined about coaches who were demanding efforts that were 'too excessive.' That particular year the negativity was especially vocal, and it's pretty easy to get sucked into that vortex when it is...even if you're normally someone who doesn't complain."

Ryan would get sucked into the vortex of negativity that year. He complained to any coach who would listen and grew irritable with training in general. Even the SEC Freshman of the Year was capable of being pulled into others' negativity. Negative words and attitudes are powerful forces and can derail even the most resolute of minds. Ryan was not immune to negativity and Coach Troy knew that. Ryan's father ended up calling Coach Troy to hear the coach's side of the complaints.

"I hear you're pushing the boys pretty hard, Gregg."

"Steve, it's nothing they can't handle. It's nothing they can't accomplish," responded Gregg.

"I hear ya...I just got Ryan calling me and..."

"Let me stop you there," interrupted Gregg, "Steve, if you were called by a parent on your team and they were complaining that their kid thought they were being pushed too hard, what would you say?"

After a long pause, Steve said, "Alright, alright. You got me. I'd probably tell 'em to can it. But what do you want me to tell Ryan then?"

"Tell him to trust his damn coach and do the work," responded Gregg.

The veteran coach and father (of one of the soon-to-be greatest swimmers ever) said what every Age Group coach wishes their team parents would say, "You got it, Coach. I'm with you."

With that, Steve hung up and relayed the message to Ryan. Not a word was ever spoken between Troy and Ryan about the conversation; instead, Ryan went back to work. He was soon racing like no one had ever seen.

Going to the Well

"One of the most remarkable differences between Ryan and anyone else I'd coached until that point was his ability to 'go to the well.' By that I mean, if we were running Gator Mountains[2] in the stadium and we challenged the group to do it under a minute, he'd

2 Gator coaches aimed to improve aerobic endurance by asking swimmers to walk, jog, and sprint up the stadium steps of the Swamp. Often done on intervals, completing one trip up the 90 steps of the eastern bowl was considered "one Gator Mountain." Every UF swimmer has a Gator Mountain story...just ask them.

go charging up there even if he knew he had 19 more to do. If we asked him to go 'all out' in the pool, he didn't need an explanation. He would actually put all the energy and effort he had into that one repeat. Then he'd come back and reload. He doesn't know how to save up energy for a final effort; he's full bore when he's training well," Coach Troy recalls.

When asked about his ability to perform "all out" repeats with honesty and how that developed as a character trait, Ryan points to his freshman year and the advice of his coaches. "I actually listened to what the coaches would say. They'd tell me in the middle of sets how everyone is tired. Everyone wants a break. You just have to dig deep inside and there's always something leFort" Taking the advice to heart, Ryan worked on his ability to draw from the well of energy during the harshest and most fatiguing of sets and workouts. "Once I was able to do it myself, and able to use that knowledge that everyone around me was hurting equally, I turned that into energy. At first, I was only able to do it once every other week. Then it was once a week. Then it was once a day. Then after a while, it was once a session. Then it was every repeat I wanted for a while. It was just because of Troy's words and realizing it's all about 'how bad do you want it?'"

Ryan likely would have been known as the most versatile and talented swimmer ever if he'd been born in any other generation. One particular athlete, named Michael Phelps, would continually push Ryan for that title and would be a specter over his training, egging him on to faster and faster times for the majority of his career. With the two men routinely vying for the same spots on national teams, the drive and impetus to perform at practice was always there.

As an undergraduate student at the University of Florida, Ryan would go on to experience unheralded success:

- SEC Champion, SEC Freshman of the Year, SEC Swimmer of the Year, SEC Male Athlete of the Year

- NCAA Champion, NCAA Swimmer of the Year, 24 time All-American

- 2004 U.S. Olympian (200 & 400 IM)

- 2004 Olympic Silver and Gold medalist

- 2005 World Champion
- 2006 Short Course World Champion

Photo Courtesy of the University Athletic Association

Ryan would continue to train in Gainesville under Coach Troy's tutelage for another five years because, as he puts it, "I was never satisfied. In 2007, I broke a world record and I wanted more. It made me hungry. I had to find different ways to make myself better. Troy was always able to push me in different ways. Whether it was through new practices, new sets, talking before or after workouts, or whatever, I was able to find ways to keep moving and to keep getting better." Even though Gainesville began to feel smaller and smaller for the Gator superstar, the O' Dome pool and Coach Troy's domain never lacked novelty.

Photo Courtesy of the University Athletic Association

After more than a decade of training in the same location and under the same coaching staff, Ryan, with the encouragement of Coach Troy, made a major change in his training regimen. In the lead up to the 2016 Olympic Games, he moved to Charlotte, North Carolina, to work with Team Elite and Coach David Marsh. "I was really beginning to feel like a big fish in a small pond," remembers Ryan. "I just needed a change."

CHAPTER SEVEN

BREAKING DOWN THE UF SWIM AND DIVE PROGRAM UNDER COACH TROY

Recruiting: This Ain't No Horse and Pony Show

Recruiting in the NCAA system is like a production of *Hamlet*. Everyone knows the lines, everyone knows the basic tenants of the show, but each program puts a different spin on the final product. Programs typically have Head Coaches spend time with recruits on Friday afternoon during practice and Saturday morning during the game day workout. Recruits will walk the deck and talk to the entire coaching staff, hearing all about the services and amenities offered at that university's program. The actual workout the team does that afternoon ranges based on program, but most like to highlight the jovial and fun atmosphere to entice hesitant high schoolers who might be a bit star struck away from home.

Typically, college programs plan recruiting weekends around the incoming athletes to provide them the "optimal" visiting experience, which often includes an unrealistic view of what attending a university is *truly* like. Schools have been known to play games and run silly competitions off the diving boards at the end of Friday afternoon practices to show potential commits how "fun and dynamic" the team is. Recruits don't find out until their freshmen year that the games and fun are just a facade, and more of a "horse and pony show" put on to entice the high school visitors.

Coach Troy, however, saw recruiting in a different light. Gregg figured early on that coaching collegiately would be different for one major reason—he could, essentially, choose who came into the program; whereas, at Bolles and Fort Myers, he had to make do with whoever walked through the front door. Now, by basically interviewing athletes and putting them through low level tests, he would know what kind of athlete he was actually dealing with before they ever trained at the University of Florida.

Being recruited by Coach Troy was unlike any experience the majority of high school recruits went through. He firmly believes that college coaches have one priority—the swimmers in the water and their *current* team. "One in the hand is worth two in the bush," is the phrase that comes to mind. Friday afternoon in the O' Dome pool is known as "Friday Flyday." Every single member on the University of Florida varsity teams swims butterfly, the more grueling of the four strokes, regardless of their primary events or stroke. The exhausting afternoon of swimming butterfly in various forms isn't meant as punishment, at least not entirely. Reminiscent of Herb Brooks's[3] philosophy, if everyone on the team is complaining about the same workout, they have something to bond over collectively. Walk-ons aren't exempt from Friday Flyday; long distance swimmers don't get to miss Friday Flyday, and the group considered the most pampered, the sprinters, don't get to skip Friday Flyday. The equalizing effect of

---

3 Herb Brooks, the Team USA hockey coach in 1980, brought together collegiate players rather than NHL All-Stars to defeat the U.S.S.R. team, which was believed to be unbeatable. By running grueling practices, the players were united in one common cause driven by angst against their own coach. The common factor brought together men who otherwise wouldn't have played well together.

the end of the week workout was pretty interesting. And, *that* is the workout most prospective recruits see first!

Gregg believed in making sure the athletes he had in the water were the athletes who received his attention first and foremost. That's not to say recruits were left unattended; assistant coaches, trainers, weight room coaches, and alumni made their rounds, attending to each recruit. But the Head Coach stayed deeply immersed in the job he did best—coaching. Gregg saw this paradigm as the first of several small, low-grade tests for the recruits. Any prospect who needed to be pampered into believing that swimming for a perennial, top 10 nationally ranked, Division I program consisted of regular games and shenanigans, was *not* the kind of athlete who would fare well in an environment that demanded daily competition. Recruits who valued adulation from strangers over the commitment and intensity of their coach-to-be did not belong in a program where independence and self-motivation were paramount.

The other oddity of being recruited by Coach Troy came in the form of individual meetings in his office. Coach Troy's office donned ample physical proof of his commitment to excellence and his proven track record of results. The careful arrangement of the awards and framed mementos that covered the walls and shelves suggested that they were originally laid out by a motherly director of operations or his own deeply caring wife, but the fine layer of dust perpetually coating their surfaces pointed to their owner's ambivalence toward their existence. Gregg Troy didn't care about the trophies; he held his stock in the hard work behind them.

High school recruits were allotted time to come sit on Coach Troy's cushy black couch, which had a tendency to make you feel like you were sinking to the floor and far below his line of sight. Each recruit would spend time asking questions and gathering Coach Troy's opinion as to how they would fit into the program—*not how the program would conform to what the recruit had done previously.* Each question that potential commits asked was always answered with one underlying constant. Coach Troy replied with the truth, regardless of potential fallout from the answer.

Honesty

Chris George was a standout distance swimmer from the Jacksonville area. As a Bolles athlete who trained under Coach Jeff Poppell, one of Coach Troy's Head Age Group coaches, Chris understood how to work hard. After a state runner-up finish in the 500 Free (4:32.00), he showed potential to be a strong collegiate swimmer. At 17, Chris went through the recruiting process and had narrowed his options down to the University of Florida and the University of Pittsburgh. Chris was an intelligent student athlete and had aspirations to work in the medical field, as his father had. He knew both schools would provide a balance of academics and athletics, though the balance would prove to be different at each institution.

Chris, while enamored with the idea of being a Gator, was taken aback at the blunt honesty from Coach Troy in a one-on-one meeting that followed a great recruiting weekend. "He told me point blank that my speed was lacking, and I would struggle to make travel teams and conference teams because there were only so many points pure distance guys could add. He said he was happy to have me on the team and he would be happy to offer me a scholarship worth the cost of books, but he really pushed me to consider going after my academic goals at Pitt. He knew I'd do well on the team up there because of my work ethic, but he knew it was probably more appropriate for me to attend Pitt for academics."

After finishing 10th at the 2004 Olympic Trials in the 1500-meter freestyle and years of competing for Pitt, Chris found his way back to the pool deck through coaching. Becoming a successful coach in his own right, Chris would assist Jeff Poppell, at Gulliver Preparatory School in Miami, Florida, before taking over as Aquatics Director and head coach of the team. His career has already seen him lead multiple teams to State Titles and athletes to international success. As he helps guide athletes toward appropriate college programs, Chris remembers the honesty Coach Troy afforded him. While supporting those athletes, he says, "I regularly think to myself. *What would Coach Troy say?* I want to offer my swimmers the foresight and vision he had with me. He saw that I valued my education and he was looking out for me, even though I didn't know it. He knew

I would have more opportunities and a different experience at Pitt, and I'm grateful he helped me see that."

Coach Chris George, Aquatics Director, Gulliver Preparatory School
Photo Courtesy of Carolina Milano Photography

Mike Joyce, an eventual All-American and top eight NCAA finalist in the 400 IM, also rehashes a forthright conversation with Coach Troy. "I wasn't even on the recruiting radar for Coach Troy. My coach and Gregg had talked about me, and I called Coach Troy basically begging to be allowed to swim at UF. He told me pretty bluntly that I wasn't fast enough to make travel teams and would have to work my butt off just to keep up." That brazen honesty was a double-edged sword for Gregg and the Gators.

Coach Troy believed if athletes couldn't bear to hear the truth over the phone or out of the water in a calm, introductory meeting, there was no way they would be able to accept truths about their swimming in the heat of the moment during an intense workout. Troy had spent decades pushing and testing athletes in Fort Myers and Jacksonville. He knew the pressure points to push and the phrases to use to determine which high schoolers were capable of being challenged, pushed, and driven to accomplish more. He also knew teenagers couldn't be trusted to be gritty if they responded in certain ways to small bits of adversity. Being told, "You aren't good enough to achieve your goals doing the work you're doing now. You're going to have to work a lot harder," is not easy for high school athletes who have been told "how talented they are" by their parents, friends, and local competitors for years.

Often the big fish from small ponds across the country would sit on Coach Troy's black couch and wait to hear how they would be offered half or full scholarships, immediate positions on travel teams, or the best locker in the locker room upon their arrival. Coach Troy was able to differentiate the wheat from the chaff by telling those recruits, "You'll likely not make a travel team your freshman year. You'll have to fight to be on B or C relays. You'll work harder than you've ever worked; but if you come, I think I can offer you a scholarship equivalent to the cost of your books." The ones who lacked grit or felt entitled deflated slightly and usually asked questions like, "Oh, I won't travel or make the conference team right away? You can't offer me more money?" Those who saw an opportunity to work and improve usually steeled themselves before nodding in agreement and saying something along the lines of, "Ok. I can work toward that. If I improve a great deal and score points at meets you designate, can my scholarship be increased in coming years?" Those type of growth mindsets were the rough diamonds Troy hoped to cut and polish.

These were the types of athletes who could be trusted to go the extra mile at UF, figuratively and literally. Mike Joyce, now an Auburn University Assistant Coach, recalls, "He pushed me hard after allowing me on the team. He made me lead lanes in warm up for guys who were much faster than me. He told me regularly that I wasn't good enough for the goals I had based on the work I was doing. Eventually, his words

Mike Joyce, Assistant Coach,
Auburn University
Photo Courtesy of Mike Joyce

caught up to me. Something in me just snapped after my freshman year and I set out to prove to him, and to myself, that I was capable of doing the work he put in front of me. As a coach now, I think it's really hard sometimes to be as honest as I remember him being with me, but I know it's what is right and try my best to emulate that."

Coach Troy didn't lie to recruits and tell them they'd make the travel team, or that "they'd fit right in" and would be able to ease into the workload because, just as the UF swimming and diving weight room coach, Matt Delancy, was fond of repeating, "Division I swimming isn't for everyone!" Typically, it wasn't the yardage that made Florida swimming tough. It wasn't the weight room workouts, or the dryland, the class schedules, the recovery sessions, or the study halls. It was the aggregation of those components that broke weaker athletes. The repetitive production of all out best efforts in the weight room, then at the pool, then in the classroom, then at the pool again, then at study hall day in and day out for weeks on end—all while being observed, critiqued, graded, ranked, and pushed—required gritty, obstinate, and mentally strong student-athletes. Being recruited by Coach Troy was an interview for a job that would demand a willingness to be pushed beyond your comfort zone, and certainly beyond any level you thought you could reach before. UF commits may have felt physically small enveloped by Troy's black leather couch, but they would walk out of that office feeling 10 feet tall, ready to take on the nation, and in some cases, the world.

What About the Athletes Who *Were* on His Recruiting Radar?

Aside from Troy's honesty and ability to identify effective pressure points, other characteristics stick out for some of the more talented international athletes choosing to attend the University of Florida. At 17, Sebastian Rousseau was a member of the 4 x 200-meter freestyle relay for South Africa in Beijing. He'd recently swam a personal best in the 200-meter butterfly and was ranked third in the world for the event when he made the decision to further his education at an American university. Sebastian didn't originally plan to leave his home country, but he sought a new challenge, and after careful deliberation he made the decision to venture stateside.

As Sebastian weighed his options on which school to attend, the University of Arizona and the University of Georgia topped his list. These schools boasted top-notch swimming programs and offered a small South African contingency, an enticing draw for a young man almost 8000 miles from home. Ultimately though, it was over dinner at Ballyhoo's, a local Gainesville haunt frequented by the swimming team, Coach Troy won over Sebastian's trust and future.

"I sat down with him (Troy), and I think before our appetizers even arrived, he had a plan for me laid out. He knew which international meets I would swim, when I'd rest, when I'd taper for SECs or NCAAs, and he seemed to know my path to London 2012," recalls Seb. "Nothing was beyond my capability; he wasn't just telling me what I wanted to hear." What drew Rousseau to Coach Troy was a level of planning and assuredness that the other schools had lacked. While Dr. Dave Salo at the University of Southern California and Coach Jack Bauerle at the University of Georgia have had their fair share of planning for international swimmers, Coach Troy's true love for what he does and passion comes through in ways that resonate with athletes. "I ended up committing to UF because I knew Coach Troy's track record with Ryan and others and because of the faith I had in Coach Troy and the Gators' coaching staff. I believed they believed in me," Seb agrees.

As Coach Brent Arckey of the Sarasota Sharks had to say on Coach Troy, **"He is very good at taking risks on people who want to do something great."**

Coach Troy and Seb Rousseau/Photo Courtesy of Seb Rousseau

Planning: Seasons, Training Blocks, Weekly Schedules, and Daily Workouts

As he had been doing for decades, Gregg continued to plan the program's direction and training from a 30,000-foot view. He approached each year of Olympic quadrennium with a calculated purpose and seemed to think several steps ahead of other coaches.

Each year of training is broken into a short course season and a long course season. Short course meets are conducted in 25-yard pools and run roughly from the end of August through the NCAA Championship meet in late March. Immediately following the NCAA championships, the long course season begins. Some programs take a week or so off to regroup and adjust after the fatigue following the magnitude of the NCAA meet, but a week without training would be sacrilegious for the unrelenting program and the truly committed at the University of Florida. Those with lofty August ambitions knew not a day could be wasted. Long course meets run in 50-meter pools and it is the most popular course set-up worldwide. The long course season prepares swimmers, leading up to either Senior Nationals or international competitions abroad in early August. Following these meets, the cycle repeats and the short course season begins anew.

The varsity short course season is often broken into different parts, called training blocks, a practice commonly replicated by most American university programs. The months of August through November comprise the first block of training which usually focuses heavily on aerobic and endurance based training. Swimmers acclimate themselves to being in the training pool and freshmen adjust to new training styles and demands of collegiate swimming. November through early December are designated for mid-season racing to accomplish two things: 1) allowing swimmers to have some fun and race, and 2) giving coaches a feel for the kind of work that remains to be done before late February and March.

December and January are typically heavy work months for most programs, though the degree of difficulty in those weeks' training varies enormously among schools and coaches. The University of Florida swimmers were known to suffer physically as much or more than teams across the country during "Holiday Training," the weeks designated for the most hellish and grueling work of the year. By eliminating the stressors of classes and study hall, Holiday Training essentially became an in town training camp. The focus is to train, eat, recover, and repeat. Unfortunately for the Gators, Florida is a top destination state for northern teams and universities when it comes to holiday training trips! For the Gators, there wasn't really anywhere for them to go that would be more pleasant or uplifting, except maybe Hawaii or the Caribbean. The notion of remaining on campus to grind at practice while almost all other UF students return home in early December presented an even greater mental challenge for most.

After two weeks of holiday training that feel like an eternity, taper season finally comes around. It is in January that teams begin preparing for conference championships. Tapers are highly individualized methods of reducing volume completed in practice, while increasing intensity and rest periods to allow athletes to compete at race speed or faster. Fine-tuning technical details and mental race-rehearsal practices are commonplace during taper periods, but there is no exact formula for the perfect taper. Each year there are several talks at many coaching clinics around the world discussing "new and improved" or "scientifically-backed" designs for the best possible taper. Coaches exchange ideas and theories, but nothing has been proven to be foolproof. The general consensus, though, is that designing an effective taper requires a combination of art and science. Feel, intuition, and concrete times are all components, and no two tapers are alike.

As one could expect, Coach Troy has his own theories about the right way to taper. "Three days or three weeks—no middle ground," was Coach Troy's tagline for the art of the taper. The larger the body, the more muscle on the body, and the more work the body had done, generally sprinters, require a longer taper. Distance swimmers and those with relatively low fast-twitch muscles kept working until three days before their first event to keep fitness and aerobic levels high. As he had learned time and time again at Bolles, each taper had individuals who needed different nuances to their rest cycles. Some needed more sleep, some needed extra weight room sessions, some needed more easy swimming, and a few needed to go even faster more often. Making those adjustments was done, seemingly, by the seat of his pants on deck; but, **those 10-second decisions were fairly certain after more than 20 years of experience**.

Swimmers weren't the only ones who learned more about the art of tapering during the last remaining weeks of the season; so did coaches. While some coaches grow restless or anxious watching swimmers do less work, Coach Troy forces himself into a state of "zen" when taper time rolls around. He characteristically is quick to tell a coach when they were being too hard or demanding; the last few days before a championship meet is no longer the time to be harping on being in the water exactly on time. If a swimmer isn't focusing on the details correctly 32 weeks into a season, they aren't going to start doing it correctly under stress in the final days! Coach Troy was specific about when he used his stopwatch, instead relying on what he saw and focusing on technical changes that could be made. Watching Coach Troy interact with swimmers and coaches in the final weeks of a season was like watching a mentalist decipher someone's hopes, desires, and secrets. Years of practice and experience, under the guidance of Troy, allowed the Gator staff to tailor each tapering period to the needs of both the group and the individuals.

Coaches' Meetings and the Lost Value of Arguing

Planning training blocks and weekly practice schedules (see insert, page 84) was both an individual and collective effort. Each coach on staff was assigned a portion of the team to supervise and direct. Groupings on the Florida team generally consisted of: sprinters, short- and mid-distance stroke swimmers, IMers, and distance swimmers. Fridays saw 200 flyers/400 IMers, 100 flyers/200 IMers, and non-flyers come together. At the onset of each week, the coaches knew which groups they'd be watching, which workouts required individualized sets, and which days were designated for team-based workouts or sets.

Weight room plans were discussed and written by the UF weight room coaches with input from Coach Troy, while dryland fell on the assistant coaches to direct and dole out to swimmers. Increases in intensity and practice adjustments were typical topics of discussion in the weekly staff meetings that took place in the second story meeting room overlooking the outdoor pool.

As former UF Assistant Coach Hollie Bonewit-Cron, now the head coach for the Miami Redhawks, remembers, "Staff meetings centered around practice goals for the week and an outline of what Coach Troy wanted to do with each group. He would give us a template for what each day centered around for the week in terms of sets he wanted to do, a skeleton of sorts, where we filled in the pieces...Gregg would describe the week to all of us and would take us through where he wanted the intensity to increase throughout the week."

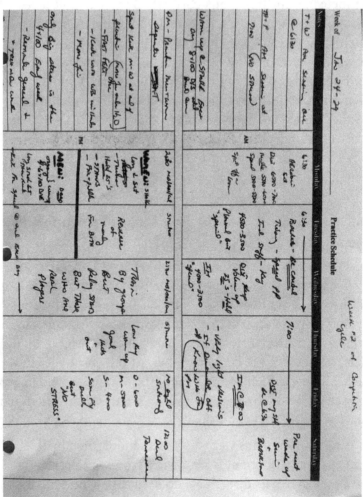

Weekly Plan; Photo Courtesy of the Author

While some staff meetings were purely informative or logistics-based, like planning travel for a dual meet or discussing plans for a recruiting weekend, other meetings were more contentious. Typical of high-achieving and task-oriented organizations, discussions regarding the direction of a group or the intention of action plans were always done behind closed doors. Back on deck, Coach Troy expected every coach to work together to achieve the goals set at the beginning of the week. Therefore, when coaches disagreed about the purpose of certain sets, the efforts of specific swimmers, or the value of mandated training styles, coaches were expected to speak up at the meetings and voice their dissent without making the matter personal.

In today's world, fewer and fewer people are capable of confronting someone face to face, in part thanks to the anonymity allowed by social media and technology. Sending a passive aggressive email is much easier than sitting across the table from someone, telling them directly that you think their plan isn't complete or is lacking components to make it successful. Coach Troy sought to hire coaches who refused to be "yes men" (or women), expecting that issues be brought up privately and timely in order to ensure the most successful path forward. Coach Martyn Wilby, associate women's head coach ('97-'17) was a self-described "devil's advocate." Coach Wilby enjoyed arguing the other side of nearly every Coach Troy argument, solely to make certain his colleague was making the best possible decisions.

That's not to say that every instance of dissent was taken under consideration. Some assistant coaches walked out of meetings frustrated, but giving his staff the space to speak their minds regardless of the outcome was key in maintaining overall cohesion in Coach Troy's eyes. Some of those frustrated coaches learned, in time, why changes were or weren't made based on their recommendations and Coach Troy's experience.

I personally found myself in situations during summer training in which Coach Troy would tell me, during warmup, to write a main set for practice. After spending the entirety of the warmup deliberating and after a few revisions, I'd write out what I thought was a fairly respectable and challenging set.

Halfway through the set, and more than halfway through my allotted time, Coach Troy would sidle up next to me on deck and slowly explain why everything I'd written was completely out of place and incorrect for the week. He'd point out areas of my set that called for efforts that were too intense immediately following a "quality" practice, which had required maximum efforts. Or, he would point out that I'd written parts of the set to include fins, when I knew that tomorrow the swimmers would be kicking 30 x 100 with fins. The lesson learned, after Coach had torn up my set midway through, reminded me a great deal of when my father handed me a chainsaw when I was 12 years old and said, "Here's how you start it. Here's how it runs. Those branches need cutting." Over several summers, I'd manage to mangle a few main sets about as badly as I mangled those branches, but such was the process of learning how to connect the dots under Coach Troy; it was about as easy as drinking from a fire hose.

As children learn the names of animals, they might associate "big, furry, and four legs" with a "dog." That is, until they are told the animal they're seeing is actually a bear. Then that same child will see another animal the next week and decide between "bear" and "dog," until they learn what a "sheep" is. That process of assimilation felt akin to my own development of skills under Coach Troy. Connecting the dots of training was vital; failing to recognize the same mistake would elicit a barrage of questions. "What was the focus last week? What is the focus the rest of this week? What will we focus on next week? How many weeks until championship season? What equipment have we used, overused, or underused?" The list is never ending. Hence, being a part of those disputed staff meetings each week was a proving ground for what you'd observed, what you'd taken note of in workouts, and whether or not you could back up your additions or manipulations to the weekly schedule as outlined by the wizard behind the curtain.

I believe Coach Bonewit-Cron described the coaching and learning experience best when she told me, "There was rarely a moment in which expectations were lowered for any reason on or off the deck. All the coaches had high expectations not only for the athletes, but for each other. Gregg would keep us all on our toes every day with everything we did. We wouldn't bitch to each other on staff, we would simply 'suck it up.'"

The "Wet Side" of Coaching

The "wet side" of coaching encompasses all aspects beyond the walls of the office. Conducting dryland sessions, writing sets, explaining technique, and implementing an efficient and productive training block are all components of the wet side. Working as an assistant coach under Gregg Troy meant fastidiously attending to all aspects of your presence on deck. Troy observed and critiqued everything from appearance to mannerisms to body language to diction and pacing to ensure each coach was extracting the maximum value from each practice.

There was never any explicit rule, but just as one would expect to see New England football players at Gillette Stadium decked out in nothing but red, white, and blue Patriot gear, Gator athletes and coaches were expected to display team pride donning orange and blue on deck daily. The first step to *feeling* like a team is *looking* like one. At swim meets, coaching cohesion was exemplified with a standard uniform—t-shirts and shorts in the morning, polos and slacks for finals. Onlookers could plainly see that the Gator coaches communicated with each other and were on the same page; they knew just by the clothes on the coaches' backs.

Cohesion among coaches didn't only happen in the public eye though. Before setting foot on deck for practice, coaches had already agreed on sets and their purposes, discussed technique and desired outcomes, and the day's intentions. The copies of the written practice from which coaches read were often annotated with comments in the columns such as, "If less than five athletes go sub 55 on number one, repeat the set until the group begins at the same point." Occasionally, though, Coach Troy would "tear up the practice completely based on something he saw from the group," as SEC Champion Seb Rousseau notes. His ability to be flexible came from having a schedule, knowing what needed to be done, and working within those limits based on the information at hand in any given workout. From structure and discipline comes the freedom to change.

Gators typically spent four weeks at the start of each season reviewing common drills and stroke progressions; coaches worked on building similar stroke styles and adjusted to each swimmer's individual nuances. To promote unity among coaches and swimmers, using a common language was fundamental. Nothing was more frustrating or time-sapping than coaches calling the same drill by different names; that type of confusion was never tolerated. Common diction and a bank of short, evocative phrases used to motivate and connect with swimmers in tight rest periods between intervals was important for the fast-paced workouts run by the Gator staff. It was common to hear phrases like, "Grip it and rip it!" which Gator backstrokers knew to mean, "There's no need to grab deep water. We are focusing on high-tempo backstroke for sprint purposes. Grip the water as the hands enter and rip the pull to your feet in a straight line."

Just as appearances and language unified the team and staff, a common sense of pacing, instruction speed, and body language among coaches was also important to Coach Troy. With all coaches giving instructions with the same vocabulary and sense of pacing, practices were more efficient, and no time was wasted on anything that could distract from high quality work.

Gator Time: Early is on Time, On Time is Late

Swimmers at the University of Florida were taught from their first day on the team that arriving early was a sign of respect for their teammates and coaches; tardiness was unacceptable. Swimmers knew to arrive early to receive the best possible preparation for the day's warmup and main set focus points. That meant that coaches had to arrive even earlier to beat the swimmers on deck to show their vested interest in the practice, too. Timeliness denoted respect for others and the program. Demanding swimmers arrive on time, or early, requires that coaches show equal or more dedication to the same task if they wished to retain the respect of their athletes. Coach Troy would ask assistant coaches to go down to the pool deck early to get a pulse of the team's mood and attitude. By arriving early, the coaches could collect tidbits of information on how athletes were feeling, what they were stressed about, what they were looking forward to, and more. The head coach himself would come hustling in the O'Dome doors like clockwork five minutes before practice was slated to begin. Shaking a plastic cup filled with ice and iced tea, Coach Troy was always hurried, but never rushed. Athletes seemed to instinctively know he had been rewriting and retooling the practice and working until the last possible second before arriving just in time to uphold his streak of prompt arrivals. A sense of urgency and authority hung around him like a department store cologne.

Once practice began, sets were explained quickly and without distraction. Coaches were frequently reminded to empty their hands of anything that might distract the attention of listening athletes. A spinning whistle, a brimming coffee mug, or keys jingling on one's finger can all impede an athlete's capacity to memorize the prescribed set. Coaches, often subconsciously, busied their hands while speaking and needed the reminder to present the set with minimal distractions.

On days that the practice was split by training groups, coaches divided the athletes with never more than a moment's pause. Sometimes, the sets were written on white boards, other times they were printed out on paper and slapped to the gutter for swimmers to see, but there were times the coaches simply read the sets aloud and swimmers had to rely on their listening skills. Presenting sets in various ways kept swimmers on their toes—meaning visual learners often had to sharpen their listening skills and on a moment's notice. Auditory learners had a slight upper hand, as coaches were always expected to project and be heard across the pool, regardless of the set's initial mode of presentation. Kinesthetic learners benefitted when asked to demonstrate a skill for the group, or when pulled from the pool to have their arms and hands manipulated by a coach teaching a technique skill. While Coach Troy would never use the terms "kinesthetic learner" or "auditory learner," as he finds phrases like these too academic, his time teaching and working around athletes led him to believe that teaching skills in a variety of ways was the best way to reach as many individuals as possible.

After spending only the necessary amount of time to clearly explain a set, swimmers were off. While some may look at past University of Florida practices and wonder how teams could have possibly accomplished 10,000 or more yards in just two or two-and-a-half-hours, those same observers don't understand how the UF coaches learned to maximize their time in the pool. Moments between sets were intended for taking in water, Gatorade, or electrolytes. Pauses between rounds were for instructional comments and for making adjustments for better results on the next round. Coaches did not spend extra seconds between sets and rounds to tell stories or rattle off stand-up comedy. While those stories only take up a few extra seconds, the accumulation of a few extra seconds multiple times during a practice, twice daily for several weeks over the course of a season adds up to a significant portion of time and yardage wasted.

That's not to say practices were stiff and boring. Coach Troy and the Gator staff knew the value that good music added to workouts, and speakers were often turned way up in the O'Dome. When the dial was tuned to the local country station, if you looked closely, you could catch Coach Troy tapping a foot to the beat or muttering along with the words to a Garth Brooks' song. The athletes thrived on loud beats reverberating in the rafters during hard sets.

Coaches flowed from one corner of the pool to another. If any coach stood in one spot too long, Coach Troy might give a stagnant coach a nudge and recommend they walk around to view practice from a different angle. Since swimming technique happens in three dimensions, coaches were encouraged to watch from different angles. Someone watching practice from a fixed point at the end of a lane only saw two dimensions of a stroke—height and width. By moving constantly and observing different angles, coaches were better informed on what might be creating drag or propulsion issues in a swimmer's stroke.

Just as music pumps up athletes, a coach's demeanor also directly affects the mood and performance of a group. A coach sitting in a chair an entire practice will rarely illicit the same responses as a lively and mobile coach. As a coach, leaning on the backstroke flagpole with one hand, languidly watching as swimmers go through the motions of training, while giving little to no technique feedback is a surefire way to ensure you'll receive little to no effort from your athletes. Coach Martyn Wilby, the longtime associate head coach for the Gator women alongside Coach Troy ,once said, "Every practice is a performance. You've got to think of yourself as a rock star putting on a show. No one wants to pay to go see 15 acoustic songs in a row from an artist sitting in a chair. There has to be changes; there has to be movement. Act like your guitar amp has one extra, secret volume notch. While everyone else plays at a "10," take your practices to an 11!" (Like any truly cultured person, Coach Wilby is a fan of *Spinal Tap*).

Each time coaches and swimmers wrapped up a workout, there was a variety of emotions and different levels of urgency depending on homework or class schedules. Some swimmers scurried out of practice as fast as possible to get to the dining hall, the weight room, or to their lecture across campus. Those who had frustrating practices sometimes hugged their gear bags as they skulked out, dragging their feet in frustration. Coaches occasionally whisked off to make phone calls or attend meetings, while athletic trainers went to work on those athletes who had time for recovery and injury prevention work.

Coach Troy, though, could be consistently found after practice talking with someone—an athlete, an assistant coach, whoever needed his listening ear. Sometimes the conversations were relaxed, sometimes they were animated, and sometimes they were harsh. Some athletes who had great workouts got stopped for a quick word, and sometimes he nabbed someone who was off their game. He often let the athlete do the talking, that is, until they said something that would spark a quick jab or diatribe. It was rare for Coach Troy to leave the deck before everyone else; he seemed to always find the extra time after workout to gather information from the athletes and help them adjust to whatever was coming next.

Good vs. Great: Developing Mental Toughness and Teaching Accountability

Late in a Thursday evening practice, Coach Troy unleashed one of the sets the Gators despised most: 10x300-yard repeats on a 4:30 interval with the goal of maintaining the swimmers' best possible average time. The grueling 3,000-yard set only takes 45 minutes. The yardage itself wasn't daunting to any of the Gators (with the possible exception of freshmen sprinters still acclimating themselves to the training environment), nor is the interval particularly challenging; most athletes arrived in Gainesville as freshmen having trained in high school at a much faster base interval. The set is daunting because the amount of pain and physical duress each swimmer will feel is entirely based on how hard each individual swimmer is willing to push themselves. Maintaining a 3:20 average hurts significantly less than maintaining a 3:05 average, yet committing oneself to repeatedly go faster requires a certain amount of mental toughness. The masochistic nature of the sport is clear when athletes undertake "best possible average" sets.

High achieving, resilient athletes will use every second of rest on the wall to physically and mentally prepare for the next repeat. They will blow bubbles forcefully at the surface of the water to lower their heart rates at a faster rate, they will use positive words to encourage themselves and their teammates, which in turn increases serotonin and improves physical performance, and they will mentally refocus their attention to single out which details to improve on.

Those who have not yet been taught how to handle adversity and those who are not at their grittiest will find excuses to dampen their performances. Each repeat will exacerbate their negative outlook, weighing them down like a poorly packed trailer. With attention focused on self-deprecating thoughts, there is no attention left paid to minute details which could positively affect performances. Flip turns widen, underwater kicks become slow and ineffectual, breaths take longer, and average times balloon. One of the reasons Coach Troy loves "best possible average" sets so much is because they simultaneously boost swimmers who understand the set while highlighting those who need help developing grit and mental toughness. This particular set, when it was delivered in late January, was the ultimate learning experience for one athlete who needed to work on her resilience and growth mindset.

April,* who had been a stellar high school competitor in the state of Florida, was a soon-to-be NCAA qualifier for the Florida Gators. Before she arrived at UF, April was the best swimmer on her club and high school teams by a long shot. The only meets where she had true competition were the FHSAA state meet in early November and the national level meets she attended in March and August. At her routine workouts and local bi-monthly racing opportunities, though, she was largely competing against herself and her own best times.

Stepping from her limited environment into a large Division I program with a history of finishing in the top 10 at the national level was a shock to the system for the sheltered athlete. This experience wasn't unique to April though, often freshmen athletes struggled to adjust to life outside their bubbles. No longer were parents telling them "how great" and "how talented" they were. Coaches expected each athlete to compete in each practice as if they were competing at their end of season competitions. "It's just practice," was no longer an acceptable response to slow daily times. "There's no one to race," was an even more laughable excuse, as everyone in the pool was at or above national standards.

April, for whatever reason, was having a poor practice on that late January day. Elite athletes are still human; they have drama with boyfriends and girlfriends, they have trouble with classes and grades, and they are sucked into family issues even from a distance. At the highest levels of sport, coaches work to numb athletes from the outside world and teach them to compartmentalize those issues, focusing only on developing athletically as much as possible each session. So, while April was having a poor practice and couldn't seem to get up to speed, Coach Troy watched and observed.

As the set of 300s progressed, and April's times remained stale, Coach Troy mentally recalled the goal meeting he'd just recently had with April. Just days prior, April had sat in his office explaining that she was aiming for NCAA time standards and hoped to be considered for relay positions in mid-February at the SEC meet. Those kinds of statements were like lighter fluid to Coach Troy. Casually sprinkling in hopes and dreams and goals for swimming around Gregg is vehemently cautioned against—unless you are willing to back up those goals with your time, effort, and willingness to learn. Saying, "I'd like to..." was waving a checkered flag in Coach Troy's mind, a signal to begin helping you as only he knew how.

After April's ninth unbearably mediocre 300, I was pulled aside. As a manager and learning coach, I'd been told to purchase a stopwatch and always have it handy just in case I could be of use. Coach Troy bore down on me as I stood over three lanes in the corner of the shallow end. Pointing at me, he grumbled, "Take out your stopwatch. Be ready." I fumbled with my pocket and set down the clipboard I'd been using to record averages.

As swimmers finished the last of the 10x300s, assistant coaches began calling out the warm-down set. Coach Troy barked at several swimmers inhabiting April's lane, telling them to clear out. April tried slinking under the lane line with the group.

"No! Not you," Coach Troy told her. Returning to her lane, with an almost undetectable eye-roll only visible to me, April adjusted her suit straps and looked up at Coach.

"Darling, I'm going off what you told me just a couple of days ago. But if you think averaging 3:12's—which is 1:04's PER ONE HUNDRED—is going to cut it, you're out of your mind. We are going to need someone who can go 1:46 or better just to sneak into the B final at NCAAs! The time of 1:45 is going to be the slowest split on the 800 free-relay! And you're over here, going third in a lane of people who have no business going in front of you, hiding in a pack of mediocrity!"

He was right. The math simply doesn't lie. A 3:12 average was just training her to go back and forth, she wasn't working toward going faster. Knowing Coach Troy was right didn't make the next statement out of his mouth any easier to grasp for April though.

"You're going to redo this set. Right now. You're a grown adult. You can leave anytime you want. But someone aiming to be an NCAA qualifier shouldn't leave this deck until she's done at least ten 300s under 3:06. Anything less is just lip service to 'I want to be great.'"

I stood half frozen. Ten more sounded daunting, and I wasn't even swimming them! April glared at us and put her goggles on with an attitude. "Right here, on top," Coach Troy gestured. As the digital clock climbed from :55, to :56, to :57, I watched April set her face into a grimace of determination. She pushed off the wall with more force than I'd seen on any of the repeats in the last 45 minutes.

Over the course of 12 laps, April's tempo had slowed back down to what she had been holding. Physiologically, it would be tough to jump start her muscles to move faster. She two-beat kicked her way into the wall with a 3:09. It was the best time she'd gone all practice, but it wasn't 3:06. I called out the time loud enough for only her to hear, but the water splashing at the gutter made it incomprehensible for Coach Troy, who sat on the far edge of the pool watching. He raised his eyebrows at me, as if asking for the time. I held up nine fingers and he threw his chin in the direction of the bulkhead, signaling for another. As Coach Brent Arckey, one of Coach Troy's former assistants, and current national team coach, knows, "He definitely can see in people some things that they don't see in themselves at the time." Coach Troy knew April had more gas in the tank; she just wasn't willing to go to that level of self-inflicted pain herself.

I stood over the girl; she was just a few years younger than me, someone I would probably see in class tomorrow. Feeling conflicted, I said, "Gotta go again, you weren't under." With a hard snort from her nostrils, April was off again. After a couple more misses, each promisingly closer to the 3:06 mark, Coach Troy sauntered back over. I took a breath of relief, thinking it was over. He sat on the diving block in the lane next to hers and said, "3:08 isn't 3:06. If you can physically get that close, you can get under. You're holding yourself back. You feel sorry for yourself, and you're allowing this. Good is 3:08. Great is under 3:06."

Tears welled at the edge of her eyes, but April put her goggles back on. By this time, the pool was clear. Her teammates had left, and April was, technically, free to go as well, but she knew Coach Troy was right. She knew she'd been content with her excuses during the set, and she wasn't going to give Coach Troy the satisfaction of seeing her cry. April exploded off the wall with even more force than before.

She hit 1:01 at the 100-yard mark...a 1:02 split at the 200-split...1:03 on the last one—her first 3:06! I loudly called out the time so Coach Troy would hear it; he allowed himself the smallest of smirks before saying, "Only nine to go..." April looked at me and I looked at her. She was up to fifteen 300s as it stood, 9 more?! I looked at my stopwatch, then at April. With a newfound fury and fire in her eyes,

April was gone by the next 30 second mark. She rattled off five more 300s under 3:06 before Coach Troy got up from his seat on the ledge by the side of the pool.

"Someone who can knock out six 300s in a row under 3:06 after doing 15 at 3:12 is capable of having gone that fast from the beginning of the set, do you understand?" Coach Troy asked April. She nodded. It was a painful lesson to have learned physically, mentally, and emotionally, but mediocrity wasn't going to serve anyone with national level goals. The extra repetitions might be labeled by some as harsh, and it's true; the lesson was harsh.

But in February, April made the SEC team. Then her performances earned a spot on the NCAA team and a spot on Florida's NCAA relays. It is possible she could have swum just as fast without having done a total of 25 300s that night, but she wouldn't have become nearly the same mental giant and person of great fortitude she did.

Summer Training in Gainesville

Following the conclusion of each spring semester, swimmers were faced with a decision. While most college students pack their dorm rooms and make plans to travel, work summer jobs, or head home for rest and relaxation, dedicated swimmers are faced with choosing where they'll train for the long course season. Sometimes that decision was out of their hands.

As has been the style for decades, college swimmers generally prefer to stay at school over the summer for training purposes. Some schools encourage student-athletes to find internships, or to return home, but most of the Gators during the Troy era knew their best environment for improvement was in the O'Dome surrounded by swimmers with similar goals and mindsets. In Gainesville, they could continue lifting weights with world-class coaches in a state-of-the-art facility, they could train with the same dryland equipment they had grown accustomed to, and, reminiscent of Holiday Training, they could treat life like a mini-training camp: eat, train, recover, and repeat! Club teams back home lacked the 25,000 square foot weight room the Florida campus boasts, and many teams only had a few athletes with times that would challenge the UF swimmers.

In a different vein, returning home would mean losing the freedom they'd gained by moving out of their family house and out on their own.

Most athletes who stayed in Gainesville took summer classes to fill the time between workouts, some found part-time work for extra cash, but others stayed in town solely to train. "It just makes sense that college-aged kids, who are more physically mature and more emotionally mature, want to hang out with their peers rather than with a bunch of high schoolers," commented Coach Troy when asked about coaching a few select college kids who returned home to train with him when he was leading Bolles. However, not everyone was always welcome to stay for the entire summer to train in Gainesville.

Coach Troy was selective in allowing only swimmers with true commitments to improving the opportunity to remain in town. Due to NCAA guidelines, college teams were limited in the number of hours they could demand of athletes. By training as part of club teams, college athletes were able to practice as much as they liked without fear of retribution from the NCAA. Troy knew that for some, staying in Gainesville was just an excuse to continue being away from parental guidance and that unfocused student-athletes would just prove to be a distraction. While there are fewer students on campus, the local bars and cantinas don't close down for summer. Coach Troy knew those without an imperative need to improve would quickly find distractions on University Avenue, Gainesville's lively bar and restaurant avenue that ran parallel to campus. Late nights in the Grog House or at Cantina 101 weren't conducive to elite level preparation, and summer training was designed to elicit the best possible development leading into the last summer months, when U.S. Nationals and international meets took place.

Seb Rousseau, three-time South African Olympian, remembers, "Back home, my coach was a Hungarian and a real straight shooter. He told you when you weren't any good and didn't hold back. Coach Troy was exactly like that, so we meshed with our similar levels of intensity. I pride myself in having always held myself to the strictest and highest of standards as a trainer, and I know Coach Troy did the same." Summers were a time of year for athletes like Seb to come together and work without distraction. "Troy had this ability to write sets that would mimic what you were going to feel in a race, and we got a lot of those over those summer months."

The tradition of inviting some to train under the Gator Swim Club team banner and purposefully sending some varsity athletes home over the summer months was a successful method and was repeated because of the production that isolation created.

As the 2013 U.S. Open Championship High Point winner that summer, Seb can speak firsthand of summertime results. Seb was the swimmer that summer who accumulated the most points with the greatest number of top eight finishes at Nationals. Following months of dedicated training and being pushed daily by his teammate, Connor Signorin, Seb remembers enduring "grueling IM sets followed by ungodly freestyle sets." The tough work set him up to win three events, break two course records, and help bring Gator Swim Club to a second-place finish at Nationals.

CHAPTER EIGHT

THE 2010 WOMEN'S NATIONAL CHAMPIONS

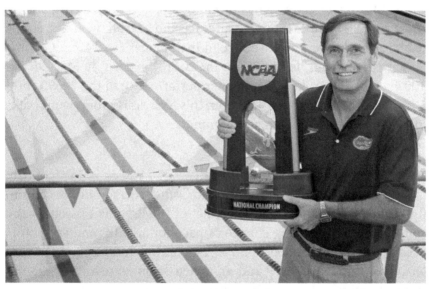

Photo Courtesy of the University Athletic Association

The Right Pieces

Former Associate Head Coach for the Gator women, Martyn Wilby recounts how the 2010 National title team was the team that "brought all the right pieces together on exactly the right weekend." A fortitudinous combination of talent, grit, devotion, experience, and self-sacrificing athletes came together for one of the most spectacular weekends of racing in Gator swimming history.

Four weeks prior to the 2010 NCAAs at Purdue University in West Lafayette, Indiana, UF Swimming had put on a memorable performance at the SEC conference meet. The Gators had raced well in this meet, one of the fastest short course yards meets in the entirety of the sport of swimming, but they had fallen short of winning. The Gators were runners-up with 126.5 points behind the University of Georgia Bulldogs but had to turn around and prepare for NCAAs.

Shara Stafford, Gemma Spofforth, Steph Napier, Sarah Bateman, Melania Costa Schmid, Jamie Bohunicky, Corinne Showalter, Jennie Smith, Elizabeth Kemp, Kara Salamone, Monica Dodson, Lindsey Rogers, Jemma Lowe, and Teresa Crippen made up the team of women who would represent the Gators on the national stage. Of those 14, four already were or would soon become Olympians in the United Kingdom, Spain, and Iceland; seven would become team record holders at least once in their career as a Gator. Gemma Spofforth, a team leader, was the world record holder in the 100-meter backstroke following her performance in the 2009 World Championships in Rome. Together, this tenacious group would take on all of America's top female swimmers.

The 2010 NCAA Championships

The Purdue Boilermaker Aquatic Center seemed oddly calm to first time NCAA attendees. The quiet of the Prelims sessions was a somewhat disconcerting change of pace for athletes and spectators used to the loud, raucous, and intense environment of conference championships. The fiery and animated sessions revolving around team standings at conference meets are replaced by individuals vying for personal glory and a few select teams with stronger chances to place well as a group. Most teams don't send enough athletes to NCAAs to mathematically score enough points to be in the hunt for a team title; the shift in the focus was palpable.

The first evening of NCAAs started with the 200-yard (4x50) Freestyle Relay. Each of the four athletes would race down and back, the shortest race distance in swimming. The Gators had finished the morning session in second place, only behind Stanford, and would race out of lane five that first night in finals. Shara Stafford, a 6'1" sprint specialist from Kansas, led the relay team followed by Gemma Spofforth, Steph Napier, and Sarah Bateman. Finishing just nine one-hundredths off the pool record, the Gators had captured a National title! Getting the victory in the first event was a spark the Gators would thrive on for the remainder of the meet.

Winning 200 Free Relay (Bateman, Stafford, Spofforth, Napier - R to L)
Photo Courtesy of Tim Binning

Following the relay's success, Melania Costa Schmid, a Spanish Olympian, dropped three seconds from her prelims swim in the 500 freestyle to take third in the B-final. Following suit, Gemma Spofforth would win the B final of the 200 Individual Medley with a time of 1:55.61, after dropping 1.5 seconds from her prelims swim. Stafford and Bateman were soon back in the pool for the individual 50 freestyle, where Shara would wind up 6th in the A final and Sarah would place 2nd in the B final. That electric first day would close with the 400-medley relay, 4 lengths of each stroke swam backstroke first, followed by breaststroke, butterfly, and then freestyle. Spofforth, the world record holder in the 100-meter version of this event, led off with the backstroke leg before Lindsey Rogers took over on breaststroke. British Olympian, Jemma Lowe followed with butterfly before Shara Stafford brought them home with freestyle in her third swim of the evening. The girls were half a second faster than their morning swim and would combine for a bronze medal!

Through the end of the first day, it was apparent that several major factors would be paramount to the Gators' continuing success: 1) relay performers would have to continue to swim for each other and race beyond their perceived abilities, 2) the most talented female athletes would have to continue to perform at their best every time they touched the water, and 3) swimming faster at night than they did in the morning session would be necessary to climb the ranks.

Luckily, the season's training had reinforced the concept of repeating efforts at maximum intensity with very little rest. The seasoned veterans leading the charge had experienced meets of equal or higher caliber. Coach Troy had prepared for the back-to-back finals swims by providing racing sets throughout the season that afforded little to no rest. Not much was going to shake the confidence of these young ladies.

The second evening of NCAAs showcased eight events: the 200 Medley relay, the 400 Individual Medley, the 100 Butterfly, the 200 Freestyle, the 100 Breaststroke, the 100 Backstroke, 3-meter diving, and the 800 Free relay. Florida had several swimmers racing to score at the top of their respective finals, but no one was certain it would be enough to be in the top five at the end of the session.

With relay points valuing double those of individual events, starting off the evening with a strong statement in the 200 Medley relay was crucial. Spofforth, Rogers, Lowe, and Bateman combined for another bronze medal with a 1:37.01 (six-tenths faster than their morning swim). Coach Wilby stood at the end of the warm down pool ensuring each athlete loosened down an appropriate amount. Wilby normally joked around with the athletes coming from the racing course and always had an enormous smile and a few words of wisdom to redirect them. But tonight, Coach Wilby was still fighting off an illness from the night before and looked much more wooden. Nevertheless, the warm down pool was his domain and he stood watch to ensure warm downs were completed in their entirety. Athletes typically like to skip parts of warm down in favor of just sitting with friends or standing in the locker room showers. But Wilby and the rest of the Gator staff knew the performance value of properly flushing lactate and stayed vigilant to ensure the swimmers were recovering properly between their races this weekend.

Teresa Crippen, a Germantown Academy product of the legendary Philadelphia-area coach, Dick Shoulberg, was up next to race. Teresa was no stranger to elite swimming. Two of her older siblings were USA National team members; Maddy Crippen had qualified for the 2000 Olympics in Sydney in the 400-yard IM, and Fran Crippen was a distinguished open-water swimmer. But before Teresa could race, her older sister Claire was in the B final. Teresa had to sit in the ready room, listening to the heat before her as her sister pushed herself to a second-place finish in the B final. Four and a half minutes after Claire's heat began, it was Teresa's turn. Finishing in 4:02.91, Teresa beat out Katinka Hossu of USC for a 2nd place silver medal. Katinka, over the next 10 years would accumulate over 100 FINA World Cup medals, several Olympic medals, world records, and the moniker "Iron Lady," for her rigorous meet lineups. Tonight, though, Teresa Crippen was the iron lady.

Jemma Lowe continued the success with a solid 5th place finish in the B final with a 52.75 and Melania Costa Schmid followed suit with a 7th place finish in the B final of the 200 Freestyle. The 100 breaststroke was the only event of the evening to see no Gator finalists or points.

Gemma Spofforth bolstered the dearth of points, though, with a blistering 50.92 100-yard backstroke, which won the gold medal. Eager to contribute to the team's success, Coach Donnie Craine and his divers, Kara Salamone and Monica Dodson, stood poolside ready to jump, flip, twist, and *not* splash their way to some points. Kara Salamone climbed the steps to the 3-meter platform, and, over the course of six dives, would accumulate 326.75 points for a solid 6th place finish. Both divers would get another chance to final the next day in the 10-meter platform prelims.

Gemma Spofforth wins the 100-yard backstroke; Photo Courtesy of Tim Binning

The end of the session came in the form of the most grueling relay in the NCAA format. The 800 free relay consists of four athletes each swimming a 200 freestyle (eight lengths of the pool). As the leadoff leg, Shara Stafford would extend herself in the 200 freestyle, the longest distance she usually raced. As a pure sprinter, she would squeeze out every last ounce of speed she possessed for the longest sprint in swimming before Jamie Bohunicky, a freshmen and hometown girl from Gainesville, would take over. Following Jamie, Teresa Crippen and Melania Costa Schmid would wrap up the day's competition for a bronze medal and 7:01.53 final time.

Saturday evening marked the sixth and final session of the 2010 NCAA Championships. The session would begin with the longest event offered, the 1650-yard freestyle, also known as "the mile." Olympic freestyle specialist Melania Costa Schmid would hold just under one minute average splits per every 100 yards for a mile to close with a 16:01.72, a 7th place finish.

Gemma and Teresa would race each other in the A final of the 200-yard backstroke. After a fantastically tight finish, Gemma and Teresa placed 2nd and 3rd, respectively. Gemma touched the wall at 1:50.24, and Teresa was just seven-tenths behind with a best time of 1:50.99; both girls would go under the pool record, but unfortunately neither would be fast enough to catch Kateryna Fesenko from Indiana.

Sprint-star Shara Stafford dropped time from her prelims swim in the 100-yard freestyle with a 47.81, moving up a spot for a 4th place finish. The Gators' momentum would stall slightly with no scorers in the 200-yard breaststroke that immediately followed. The two events, the 100 freestyle and 200 breaststroke, gave Teresa Crippen just enough time to warm down and shake out some lactate that had accumulated in her muscles during her extraordinary performance in the 200 backstroke. She was back in an A final with the 200 butterfly and she was accompanied again by a fellow Gator, Jemma Lowe. The two Gators would go 1:53.90 and 1:54.05 in the event yielding 5th and 6th place finishes. From prelims to finals, they maintained their 5th and 6th place seeds. The race was extraordinary for another reason, as well. The A final saw six women, including

Teresa and Jemma, go under the pool record set in 2005 by butterfly great, Mary DeScenza.

With only two events remaining, Platform diving and the 400-yard freestyle relay, scores were extremely tight. Stanford, UF, and Cal-Berkeley were in a tight race for first through third. Coach Craine reviewed the entry list for each of his divers, Kara and Monica, who had both made the A final. Coach Craine went over the final adjustments and hugged them each as they commenced the lengthy climb to the top of the ten-meter platform. Kara would go on to win bronze with 307.45 and Monica would finish 8th with 219.65 points. Coach Craine was proud knowing the night's overall points decision wouldn't lack help from the Florida divers, who worked extremely hard at their craft throughout the year.

Elizabeth Kemp played two major roles that weekend—one expected and one unexpected. First, Liz had kept the atmosphere light among all the girls at the hotel, during van rides, and on the deck. Coaches noticed Liz's calming effect on the team and appreciated the boost she helped provide. No one had coached her on leading with her presence, but the effect she had was duly noted. Her next major role, an anticipated one, came in the form of leading off for the Gators in the final relay. Before the four swimmers assumed their joint position behind the blocks, the coaching staff and swimmers came together one last time and the coaches told the girls, "Just go race. We'll let you all know what the points look like after. Enjoy this moment."

Another bronze medal finish to wrap up the 2010 Nat'l Championships

Photo Courtesy of Tim Binning

Following Liz's performance, Shara Stafford, on her fourth relay swim of the meet, raced second and split the fastest 100 freestyle in the entire A final field with a blistering 47.50. Gemma Spofforth, also swimming her fourth relay and 14th race of the weekend, swam third before freshman Jamie Bohunicky anchored. Seeded fourth after the morning prelims session, the Gators fought hard for a 3:13.43 overall time and another relay bronze medal to wrap up the 2010 NCAA Championships. With that final swim, the University of Florida Gators would edge out the Stanford Cardinal, 382 points to 379.5—a margin of 3.5 points. Led by Coach Troy and the University of Florida coaching staff, the Gator women had reached the pinnacle of collegiate swimming.

Photo Courtesy of the University Athletic Association

CHAPTER NINE

THE BEGINNING OF THE MEN'S SEC CHAMPIONSHIP DYNASTY

Shaping the Team

The years following the women's national title were consumed with a process that may have only been immediately apparent to Coach Troy. The success of the women's team forced all team members and contributing staff on the University of Florida teams to consider two essential questions: 1) what *helped* propel the women to the national title? and 2) what *prohibited* the women from repeating as national champs and the men from achieving the same feat?

What happened over the course of the next several years was a process described by Coach Troy as "shaping the team." While some may read the following pages and consider the process to be callous, a few items must be remembered:

- Division I swimming is *not* for every student athlete. Being a part of a perennially ranked top-10 team nationally is suitable and appropriate for *even fewer* athletes.

- The entire coaching staff, not just Coach Troy, was working from decades of combined experience to make decisions based on trends and personalities they had encountered in the past.

- Coaches are human and are governed by emotions, too. The goal as an elite coach is to override emotions as often as possible to make the most rational and helpful decisions for each athlete under your care, as well as the team as a whole.

With the nation watching to see how the Florida Gators would respond after winning a national title, Coach Troy fell back on a tried and true philosophy: *if some is good, more is better.* The women who helped win the national title were dedicated, hard-working athletes who took the time to work on their skills. Any extra time they had was dedicated to running stadiums and completing 5Ks for time. It wasn't unusual for the girls to spend thirty minutes after practice either working on specific turn skills or stroke drills between the bulkheads at the O'Connell Center, or to spend over an hour in the athletic training room working through injury prevention skills and sitting in ice baths to speed up recovery time between workouts. The coaches encouraged all athletes, male and female, to dedicate extra time to improving.

Coach Troy observed which individual characteristics helped unify the women; individual accountability and leadership were at the top of that list. While the women remained a strong group even after their national title, the men faced a troublesome pattern. The top of the men's program always showcased talented individuals who were capable of scoring at the national level (and even the international level) such as Shaune Fraser, Brett Fraser, and Omar Pinzón, but the middle of the group wasn't rising to fill in when needed. Naming captains at the beginning of the season was standard practice, but often the chosen captains held loose command over a room at best. Strong leadership is a cornerstone in running a well-adjusted team, and occasionally swimmers rise to these roles even without a captain's title. Athletes Bobby Walsh and Cameron Martin were two such men.

Active, Vocal Leadership

Between 2010 and 2012, Bobby Walsh was considered by Florida Swimming standards to be a middle of the group swimmer. Though he competed internationally for the Philippines at the 2009 World Championships in Rome, he had to work hard to be picked for travel trips and eeked out just enough results to be a part of the SEC team. Just as international success had not been an automatic qualifier for Coach Troy's attention at Bolles years ago, Bobby Walsh, the butterflier from Virginia Beach, wasn't going to garner any special attention just because of his standing on an international team for the Philippines. Previously, Gregg had coached Bobby's older brother, J.B, to a spot on the Philippines Olympic team, so he knew the mold from which Bobby was cast. Coach Troy continually pressed Bobby to work hard, finding ways to lead his peers and, in turn, push them to rise above their own perceived limits. Bobby, a fighter, rose to the challenge and creatively took to dryland as his domain for success.

Ben Hill Griffin Stadium
Photo Courtesy of the Author

Dryland encompasses all physical exercises swimmers perform on dry land (hence the name) aside from weight room activities. Florida swimmers are known to run "Gator Mountains" up the steps of the blazing hot football stadium. Accurately nicknamed, "the Swamp," the Florida football stadium is a sultry 96 degrees early in the morning before the sun has even hit its peak. By two in the afternoon, when the Gators typically congregate at the orange bench closest to the field, the heat is anywhere from 100 to 110 degrees, easily. Every step up the bleachers burns and the sun radiates off the metal seats without mercy. Thirty steps up, the stairs suddenly rise, and the angle increases dramatically. Quadriceps quiver as you press your hands into your knees to stagger up the remaining steps. But, Gators don't stagger; at least that's what Bobby told his teammates. "Gators run! Chest up, use your arms," he would holler zealously to the younger freshmen who listened. I know of at least two who heard him and heeded his encouragement: myself, and the eventual 2013 Captain of the SEC Championship Men's team, Cameron Martin.

While I eventually stopped swimming, I took to Bobby Walsh's leadership, and loved the concept of excelling in a specific arena within the overall program. I still apply that idea to the work I do everyday. If I couldn't be the greatest workout swimmer, why not at least be one of the best swimmers at dryland? Cameron Martin, a Clearwater Aquatic Club butterflier, heard Bobby's message loud and clear, too. Cameron and Bobby worked together well. Pushing each other and their fellow teammates was their specialty. More than once, the two flyers found themselves swimming against each other at the end of practice, competing for a spot on a travel team for a specific dual meet. Regularly, Bobby and Cam would have to cajole their teammates to join them on weekend runs or to keep up with them in the weight room by adding extra weight to their leg presses.

Once Bobby graduated, Cam was bequeathed the sole position of vocal leader. Faster swimmers may have been able to lead by example with their efforts in the pool, but Cam took to leading vocally and imposing his physical will at pre-practice dryland sessions. Volunteer assistant coaches spent all day thinking up intricate body weight exercises and TRX movements to incorporate into dryland. Not only would Cam knock out the same movements, but he would use a 15-pound med-ball, too, and cower others into joining him. Just as Suzanne Crenshaw had once gained a foul nickname for her hard work in the late '70s at Bolles, Cam found himself called the "dryland monster" behind his back for his extreme dedication to improving. Out of the water, classic of Coach Troy's hard-working leaders, Cam addressed the men on the team with a simple invitation, "I'm here to help anyone who wants to get better. Everyone else should just get out of the way." With that, the chatter ceased, and the group's dryland intensity rose up. Way up.

So, after leadership was addressed and improved, extra-curricular efforts were encouraged, and after coaches tinkered with a proven method of training success, there was only one more area left to improve.

Removing the Negative for an Overall Boost

Fishermen in the northern Pacific Ocean, searching for deep sea King crab often face a conundrum. The fishermen will be out at sea for several weeks on end, often amassing many loads over the course of those weeks. The problem for the fishermen is that after about two weeks King crab begin to die. So, crabs caught at the onset of an expedition may expire before returning to be processed at the docks. As King crabs decompose, they emit a toxin that can poison the entire tank, harming even the healthiest of crabs. The resulting, contaminated crabs are referred to as "deadloss." While no coach is callous enough to use "deadloss" as a term to describe the lowest performing or most distracting athletes of their group, the metaphorical similarities are undeniable. Just as great leaders can bolster a group or a team, a bad apple (or crab) can ruin the rest of a bunch. As a coach, it's never easy to approach an athlete who isn't cut out for the group they are in. It is difficult to share with an athlete that they're not performing at the level of the group or adapting to training at a fast-enough speed. Having to sit down with an athlete you've recruited and to explain that they will better reach their potential elsewhere is incredibly hard.

Coach Troy generously accepted walk-ons to the team for a few years leading up to the 2010-2011 season before he began recognizing a disheartening pattern. Too few walk-ons were cut out for the rigors of Division I athletics. The glory that accompanied a swimming career at UF was alluring, and the view most high schoolers had of collegiate athletics was tinted with rose colored glasses. The reality behind that glory was hours upon hours each week of dedication in the pool, topped with a rigorous course load, which is daunting to most freshmen in itself. Most freshmen athletes struggle with the combination of classes, tutoring sessions, study halls, exams, late nights completing assignments, morning practices (which are far more intense than what they did in high school, for most), afternoon dryland or weights, afternoon practice, recovery time, and then socializing! With only so many hours in a day, unfortunately, the Florida men found themselves in the company of a few too many freshmen commits who could not sustain the intensity the program required. Every practice was a battle. Every practice saw young men being challenged by international-caliber athletes—both male and female. There were several times this author can remember being lapped on a Monday morning aerobic practice and being barked at (by an Olympic female athlete who shall remain unnamed), "Get a move on, fairy boy!!" In dual meets, Florida men were expected to compete so that their times, at a minimum, were faster than the University of Florida women's team records. There was no room for days off or bad swims.

One day, the attrition rate caught up with Coach Troy, and he decided to tighten the restrictions on joining the team. At the same time, he began to put pressure on those swimmers performing at the bottom of the group. Coach Troy began to view the team as a bonsai tree that required shaping to bring out the superlative shape. Questionable walk-ons would now spend an undisclosed amount of time working out with the on-campus club Senior group. Coach Troy figured that if an aspiring high schooler was honest in saying, "I will do anything to swim for the University of Florida," he would be willing to get up earlier and train with high schoolers to drop the one or two seconds needed to even come close to racing at conference-level times. Only those mentally tough enough to continue battling for a position on the team and physically talented enough to continue improving would emerge victorious at the end of a year or so, earning their spot on the coveted UF swim team. While these walk-on requirements may seem harsh, they did, in fact, force aspiring Gator swimmers to rethink their choice of joining the team (since they didn't *actually* like getting up at 4:45 AM as college freshmen and *really* just wanted to sport the swimming merch). One or two hard-working young men did manage to make it onto the team; those were the type of athletes Coach Troy knew would contribute to the program.

Coach Troy and the UF staff also began to use "the Florida Five" as a way to compel student-athletes to confront their role on the team. The list consisted of five ways a Florida swimmer or diver could contribute to the team. After several weeks of observation, if Coach Troy felt an athlete wasn't adequately contributing in to at least three of the ways to contribute, he did what he did best—he confronted them with the truth.

The Florida Five

1) Score points at the NCAA Championships/SEC Championships

2) Be a great practice swimmer (Make others better)

3) Maintain a 3.5+ GPA

4) Help others make good decisions

5) Be fun to be around

If someone was neglecting their job in the classroom, pulling down the team's GPA, Troy would be promptly informed by a team advisor and would bring it up privately with the swimmer in question. If the situation wasn't rectified by the athlete in a timely manner, they would be placed in mandatory study halls. Sometimes, when drastic measures were needed, swimmers were held out of practice until their grades improved. If someone was spending too much time partying on the weekends and it was affecting their performance in practice come Monday, Coach Troy would address it. Swimmers were occasionally given second chances when mistakes were made, as a one-time blunder can be expected of a young adult freshly separated from parental supervision. In Troy's eyes though, second chances were often final chances. Coach Troy offered second chances to college athletes as a way of teaching life lessons which real life would not permit, but those second chances were never to be mistaken as signs of weakness or softness. Just as future bosses and supervisors would be, Coach Troy was tough on misbehavior when required.

Athletes who dragged bags behind them as they left practice were reminded to walk with pride, acting as if they were proud of their workouts, rather than leaving with poor body language as proof of defeat. Those who couldn't find ways to improve the team by improving themselves were often discouraged and blamed the coaching staff for "picking on them." Unfortunately, those swimmers didn't have the experience of the coaching staff as a whole or Coach Troy's understanding of what is required to perform at an elite level. Narrow-minded, inexperienced, disgruntled teenagers often found it was easier to abandon the team instead of adhering to a sense of discipline and structure designed to bring out the best in each athlete.

As Troy's ever rising-standards began to weed out the lowest-performing, least-contributing, or, at worst, down-right distracting member of the team, the remaining crux formed a stronger bond and learned to trust each other more. Knowing each person in the pool was committed to superior performance allowed practice to become a safe place to fail. Knowing that all members of the team wanted to see each other succeed encouraged teammates to ask each other for help with homework, exchange study tips, or with technique pointers in the weight room. As collaboration grew central to the team's culture, each individual's sense of purpose and role on the team solidified, and soon the Gators were on top.

2013 SEC Championships

What stood out most from the trip to College Station, Texas, in 2013 (aside from the actual racing) was the wind and the birds. College Station is a bit dreary; the wind whips around the campus at your heels and crows constantly crow. Everywhere you go, crows follow. The dismal setting didn't quite seem to be the ideal place for a potential fairy tale upset. From 1997 to 2012, the Auburn men hadn't lost an SEC Championship. The past three years had seen the Gators place second by just 40 points or less, but something had always stood in their way of beating out the Tigers.

At the time, as a team manager and pseudo-volunteer assistant coach, I was in charge of equipment needs at the meet (suits, caps, goggles, training equipment), along with any minor details the coaches could pass off (extra vans returning to the hotel early, video analysis, extra errands). I coached age group swimming in my spare time, and I appreciated the opportunity to witness high level swimming up close; the SEC Championship meet is a nexus of elite swimming. Teams spend months preparing for the showdown, which rotates between SEC sites. Countdowns to the meet are plastered in team weight rooms and locker rooms. Social media posts are fraught with reminders for students and alumni to support from the stands, and parent group chats coordinate team meals and T-shirt colors.

The meet itself is deafening. Teams gather in assigned locations around the pool, as do parents and supporters in spectator seating above. Pom poms, graphic T-shirts, and face paint are commonplace in the audience. Teams walk in together with a mixture of attitudes. The women typically behave as if they haven't seen friends on other teams in years, running to each other and squealing with joy. As Coach Troy once pointed out, "The more nervous a female swimmer is, the more talkative and friendly she'll act with friends before and during warmup." The men, on the other hand, act as if they are going to war. Scowls and chest beating are common; certain teams will take the long way around the deck to the locker rooms to avoid walking near select rival teams. Some men will retain facial hair as a mental ploy, hoping to intimidate competitors with their confidence. Any trace of stubble though is always gone before the start of the first session and before racing begins.

We were rolling as a team; four days had passed, and the swimming had been absolutely lights out each night. The superstar freshman, Natalie Hinds, had been fantastic and the women had been performing admirably. The men, however, seemed to have elevated to a new level. Relays were outstanding; the men had won the 800-yard free relay in 6:14.76, an automatic qualifying time for NCAA Championships. We saw great swims in the 500-yard freestyle. Three swimmers in the 200-yard IM final had given us a bump in points, and Brad deBorde's NCAA "A" cut in the 50 free was a spectacle to behold. It was incredible to think he had wanted to quit the sport completely after feeling overwhelmed as a freshman; here he was, second at SECs as a senior!

The next day, the men finished second in the 200 Free relay which rarely seemed to be Florida's strongest relay. Matt Curby's stellar relay start really helped out, though. His hop, skip, and two-footed jump off the front of the block looked like he'd sprung from a trampoline! It was the 400-yard Individual Medley, though, that packed the most punch that day. It was a statement UF/Coach Troy event: four A finalists, a B final winner, and a C final winner. I think the C final might have been the most exciting to watch with Ryan Rosenbaum's thrilling come-from-*way*-behind win; I still get chills thinking about the speed and strength of his breaststroke and freestyle legs. Marcin Cieślak, the Polish Olympian, took the 100 fly for the Gators with a strong 46.0, looking effortless as he glided across the surface of the water.

It was another 1-2 punch in the 200 free from Olympians Pawel Werner (Poland) and Sebastian Rousseau (South Africa), before we went 1-2-3-5 in the 200 butterfly! Cheers of, "It's great...to be...a Florida Gator!" broke out at the culmination of almost every heat. Not only were the most talented and recognized guys winning and placing high, but the swimmers in B and C finals were also finishing at the top of their heats and were bringing in great points, too. The onslaught of B and C final points would prove to be pivotal in the final results.

Dan Wallace Celebrates
Photo Courtesy of Tim Binning Photography

Two years after redshirting, Sebastian Rousseau was fulfilling his role as a team leader. After watching from home as the Gators lost the 4x200 freestyle relay two years earlier, Seb wanted revenge and wanted to win. In years past, Seb had watched as Conor Dwyer lead the Gators, not vocally or with loud, raucous cheers, but with his actions by scoring a heap of points with big-time performances. Sebastian had taken that lesson to heart, and he was on a silent warpath alongside fellow elite, international racers: Pawel Werner, Dan Wallace, Eduardo Solaeche-Gomez, and Marcin Cieślak.

Seb recalls, "The SEC meet was great. Not only were we all racing, but it was lighthearted and fun because of the attitude the younger guys brought. Everyone still did their job and did the tasks that Coach Nesty, Coach Steve, and Coach Troy had talked about for so long, but it was fun. We brought that discipline they always talked about and had fun doing it."

It was the last day of events and we boarded the bus to the aquatic center, ready to begin to walk into our final session. No one was actually talking about the SEC title, but everyone on the bus could sense it was a possibility. Coaches were playing their cards very close to the vest and no one seemed to reveal any emotions. With coffees in our hands and fire in our bellies, we strode onto the deck that day with the unspoken knowledge that victory *could* be ours.

Photo Courtesy of the University of Florida Athletic Association

After unloading the team gear, I stood at the pool's edge and watched the distance group flipping through pace 50s, trying to get a feel for what times they would hold in the mile that night. Alicia Mathieu and Jess Thielmann looked like machines, each with their own distinctive stroke style, but both knocking out 50s back to back to back just tenths of seconds apart (both girls would go on to hold the team record in the 1650 freestyle at various points in their collegiate careers). After zoning out for just a minute, I looked up to see Coach Troy jovially laughing on the corner of the competition pool pace lane. Holding a stopwatch on his hip with one hand, and leaning on the ladder with the other, he seemed perfectly at ease. Languidly, he called out pace for the girls getting ready to swim the 200 backstroke since it was the first event after the mile; Troy didn't like going out of order. Hearing him laugh like that, and seeing him relaxed and comfortable, I knew something was amiss. Something was off. In my years I'd known Coach Troy, meet warmup had felt like watching a conductor lead a marching band in action. Coaches had to know the swimmers they covered; they needed to memorize each swimmer's specific paces and pace structure. Everyone worked individually but also within the larger group framework. If a swimmer's first 50 in pace was done too fast or was too out of control, they'd be sent back to general warm up to collect themselves and would have to come back to try again. There was an order to how pace was conducted; the intensity was always frenetic. Nearly all the other coaches in the SEC tended to do pace in the lanes opposite the Gators to avoid the

Gregg smiling; Photo courtesy of Kathleen Troy

frenzy the Florida coaches brought to warm up. Tonight, there was a suspicious air of calm.

Coach Nesty still seemed tense, but the milers were his pride and joy, so he wouldn't relax until they'd performed well anyway. Coach Jungbluth and Coach Stancil seemed to be positively affected by Coach Troy and Coach Wilby's laissez-faire demeanors. Coach Wilby stood with other SEC coaches behind lane 6 with his arms crossed and, his pointer and middle finger on his bottom lip, holding back smirks and chuckling sporadically whilst making idle chatter.

Ashley, the athletic trainer, and I made eye contact and shook our heads in awe; this was new! Then, it dawned on me. The coaches must know this win is all but secured. The Gators were going to break Auburn's streak and win the SEC Championships for the first time in years and Coach Troy was already indulging in that glory.

Sure enough, it was another second-place finish in the 400 Medley relay followed by a top 3 finish and team record in the 1650 from Arthur Frayler, the swimmer I worked with most consistently! Back in Gainesville I had been in charge of watching distance practices almost every day, and I loved to see the distance athletes succeed. Arthur was a Germantown Academy product and, much like Teresa Crippen, he thrived on longer and harder workloads. He would frequently spend his off days on the weekend doing trail runs with me in the woods of Gainesville, just to give his conditioning an extra boost. His freestyle stroke was frenzied and thrashing; it never looked very efficient, but Arthur made it work for him. Arthur's record that night was the cherry on top of my ice cream sundae of a week.

The Gators clinched our first men's SEC victory in decades that night; 212 points separated the first place Gators and the shell-shocked runners-up from Auburn. I remember enjoying the wait as the top five team finishers and the runners up were announced. I noticed coaches removing cell phones from their pockets and pulling towels out of their bags. Quizzically I looked around before Brad deBorde grinned in my direction and said, "It's so your stuff doesn't get ruined when we jump in the pool!" A Texas-sized smile spread across my face that night in College Station.

To this day, I still have the button-down polo we wore the night we jumped in the pool following the win. Even though it's been washed at least 100 times, I still catch whiffs of chlorine that make me smile and remember the only lighthearted warm up I ever saw Coach Troy conduct.

The 2012-2013 Gators Knock Off Auburn!
Photos Courtesy of Janna Schulze

As of March 2020, the Gator men continue to extend their dynasty for an eighth straight year. The leadership and purposeful collaboration, that began with Bobby Walsh and his teammates, extended and continued with the additions of Mark Szaranek, Jan Switkowski, Bobby Finke, and arguably one of the greatest swimmers the world had ever seen, Caeleb Dressel.

Reflecting on his own experiences at SECs and winning SEC team titles, Caeleb Dressel sounds remarkably like Seb Rousseau of years past. Caeleb cites the collective suffering and tough lifestyle that came with enduring rigorous workouts, demanding academic schedules, and completing supplementary work as unifying factors in the development of the men's team. But for Caeleb, realizing his individual strengths and weaknesses were vital to his role as a leader.

"Honestly, from the moment I arrived, we just all knew our roles and what was required of each of us to win. I'm not really a vocal leader, I knew my role was to score as many points as possible. Not everyone can win every event they are entered in, so I had to do my part to help the team cause. Mark, Jan, and I knew that our job was to be bad asses when it came time for SECs and NCAAs. Our events didn't really overlap, so we knew we could do some damage points-wise. I don't want to say that's what made us friends, it's more like that's what made us even closer friends. We had a collective goal."

"The team was really set up so that each knew their role. If you weren't the best swimmer, but you had a 4.0 grade point average, Troy wouldn't fluff you up and tell you lies about how you were going to be an Olympic champion. He just wasn't going to sugarcoat anything. But what that did was make it cohesive for us. We were all in this together."

A history of success has built on itself, and acts as the driving force for Gator swimmers, even for those who aren't intentionally looking for inspiration. Each year that the Gators win the SEC title, the pressure rises to meet those expectations and reach the objective set and met by nearly a decade of teams.

Photo Courtesy of the University Athletic Association

"I knew the history of Florida and I knew the people who came before me. But I don't like comparing myself to anyone else. You think of Dwyer, you think of Lochte, Nesty, and Peter Vanderkaay was there at one point as a postgrad. There's a ridiculous amount of history, so I wanted to do my part, but never would I consider myself the best that came through Florida. I just wanted to do my part to be part of that history. I know I'm just going to be a guy smack dab in the middle of this program's history," mused Caeleb when asked about his impact on UF swimming history. With team leaders teaching future classes of Gators about that commitment and selfless devotion to the program, it's easier to imagine how the Florida men's program has sustained this high level of greatness.

It is also interesting to note, without the work Coach Troy did with Alec*, the blue-collared recruits likely wouldn't have trusted Troy or come to train with the Gators. Without the hard-nosed recruits, there wouldn't have been an established NCAA record of success that helped seal the recruiting commitment from Ryan Lochte. Without Ryan Lochte and his buy-in, the program may not have caught the attention of Conor Dwyer or Sebastian Rousseau (or an international contingent), who were key players in the Gator's commencement of the SEC dynasty. Without the

tradition of SEC wins along with the feeling of camaraderie and sense of duty that came with them, Caeleb Dressel would not have taken his talents to UF. A direct line can be drawn from *properly* coaching the underachieving kid in a group to eventually coaching the best of the best.

Photo Courtesy of the University Athletic Association

CHAPTER TEN

THE GOLDEN AGE

Dressel Arrives

The expectations of victory hung in the air, thick like Gainesville humidity, at the 2018 NCAA meet. The crowd has been murmuring for several heats, anxiously awaiting this moment. The announcer calls out each swimmer's name as they emerge from the ready room and take their places behind the blocks. The men are giants—each standing well over six-feet, lithe, and ready for action. Habitually, a few athletes slap their arms and chest to increase blood flow, while Caeleb springs up and down behind his block in his ritualistic manner, showcasing an impressive 42-inch vertical jump. Back home, the Florida Gator football coaches in the athletic weight room envied Caeleb's ability to jump and wished their own wideouts would take note.

The wild crowd watching the first night of the 2018 NCAA Championships is eagerly awaiting what they hope will be the fastest 50-yard freestyle heat in history. Lanes one through eight are filled with All-American- and international- caliber athletes. In lane five was Ryan Held, an Olympic gold medalist on the 4x100 Freestyle relay in Rio de Janeiro with Caeleb, not two years ago. Yet, tonight, Held and Dressel would be pitted against each other, racing for first place along with the six other A finalists.

Tonight Caeleb has a singular purpose. The Florida superstar senior has already won an NCAA title. Just as his coach has never settled for one form of excellence, Caeleb has his sights set beyond a mere win. Tonight, he wants to swim this event unlike anyone in history. Tonight, he wants to stretch the imaginations of what the swimming world believes to be possible.

The 50-yard freestyle is commonly known as the "splash and dash." There's nothing about the event as simplistic as its moniker, though. A combination of athleticism, skill, technique, and raw power, the 50 free is an event every swimmer wants to compete in, yet one at which few excel. The simplest of mistakes is compounded tenfold in such a short race; if even one stroke is 20 percent less efficient, or if a turn is missed by a quarter of an inch, there is no room or time to compensate for the blunder. At an elite level, where any competitor can claim victory, winning will require a flawless race. A performance for the ages will beg something even greater than flawless.

Caeleb stands next to his block, sneaking a glance at the poolside in the direction of his teammates. The consummate teammate, he takes pride in his blue and orange compatriots cheering him on. A deep inhalation follows as he centers his mind and prepares for the surge of power and speed to come. The starter blows one long whistle, and the eight men climb onto their starting blocks in response.

Crouching in a near-ready position, Caeleb is 99 percent prepared for the start. He leaves nothing to chance, needing to strengthen his grip on the block and tighten his hamstrings to be fully loaded for a forward explosion, not unlike a coiled spring. The years of box jumps beneath Ben Hill Griffin Stadium in the weight room doing posterior chain work with Matt DeLancey, the UF weight room coach, flash in his mind. Hours of work, drenched in sweat, have prepared him for this moment. Dressel focuses on the rough textured surface of the block top as he grips the edge and tenses his forearms.

The entire building goes silent and for a split second, only the hum of the massive aquatic center's air conditioning unit can be heard. No one is moving in the warm down pool. All eyes are fixed on lane four. The starter begins his command, "Swimmers...take your mark...*beep*." Instantly, cheers erupt from the sidelines, teammates of all the swimmers whoop and whistle, hoping to spur their friends on before they hit the water. Though Caeleb is tied for second with his reaction time off the starting blocks, and one of the last to actually hit the surface of the water, once underneath the placid surface, the race is all but won.

Six kicks and a half cycle later, Caeleb is already to the 15-meter mark before any of his competitors have even broken the surface for their breakout. Four strokes later, he's gained a half body length lead over the entire field. The water in front of him is what coaches call "clean," meaning no waves have disturbed the surface and the amount of drag or resistance he encounters is significantly minimal. In the world of 50 freestylers, the race is done. The lead is insurmountable, barring disaster. The question is: how fast will he go?

The scoreboard at the University of Minneapolis pool would take a half second to register what onlookers have just witnessed. The spectators have a decision to make: check the scoreboard to see the halfway split, or watch the breakout. If they choose to check the 25 split, they might miss half of the remaining lap. Those who choose to forego seeing the breakout, glance away as fast as possible, only to shake their head in disbelief. 8.74? Is it possible the pad went off too early? Before anyone can even second guess themselves, Caeleb is crashing down on to the final five yards of the race. Now, a full body length ahead of the world-class field, Caeleb slams into the wall and allows the momentum of his finish to turn his body, as he checks his time, along with the entire sea of spectators. Before anyone else finishes the shortest race in swimming, Caeleb knows he has not only repeated as National champion again, but he's done it in American record fashion while being first in history to break the 18-second barrier.

Wins in the 50 freestyle are considered "enormous" or "commanding" when several hundredths or a few tenths of a second separate competitors. Caeleb was *more than a full second* ahead of the 2nd place finisher. That kind of speed was unheard of, unseen, and unexpected—even from the fastest swimmer alive. Just a few years ago, armchair coaches had decried Dressel's commitment to the yardage-based, workhorse-oriented Gators program a "mistake" and huge "misstep." That night, no one could doubt the abilities and training of Caeleb Dressel and the Florida Gators.

Photo Courtesy of the University Athletic Association

Coaches Anthony Nesty, Matt DeLancey, Troy, and Steve Jungbluth Celebrate
Photo Courtesy of Tim Binning

That same NCAA Championship would also highlight the first time any human went faster than 40.00 seconds in the 100-yard freestyle, by none other than the Florida speedster himself. The heroics behind these groundbreaking races, though, and behind the amazing swims still to come in Dressel's young career, actually began years before that night when Coach Troy first began his recruitment of the young Bolles superstar.

Recruiting Caeleb Dressel & Being Recruited by Coach Troy

Despite taking a five-month hiatus from swimming before beginning collegiate athletics, Caeleb Dressel had his choice of schools as a high school recruit. The list included all the premiere swimming programs in the country, and Caeleb was a priority for each of them. After a few calls and conversations with coaches from other teams, and bad-mouthing Troy and the Gators, the University of Florida fell off Caeleb's list. Caeleb's father and Coach Troy spoke on the phone after the Gator coaching staff heard UF was no longer on Caeleb's list of potential landing places, but Mr. Dressel remained optimistic.

"Gregg, stay on him. I know my son, and he just needs time to think things through," Mr. Dressel reportedly told Coach Troy. Coach Troy and the UF staff continued their pursuit of Caeleb.

"Caeleb really does use time to think things through. That's apparent even in practice," says Troy. "But, at the time, we knew if he was thinking about it, we could get him to come to school. Two home trips and a lunch later, Caeleb agreed to come out for an unofficial visit." On a day-long trip, Caeleb connected with the UF men's team, especially the sprint star and team leader, Brad deBorde. Both cerebral creatures who thrive best in an empathetic atmosphere, the two athletes hit it off before the day was done. Coach Troy and the UF team had won Caeleb over.

Troy recalls recruiting Caeleb, "I was pretty straightforward. I told him he was on par with Lochte in terms of talent and ability. But, I also told him I thought he was more than a sprinter. He was more than a one trick pony. I knew he could be pretty dynamic in several events, so I just asked him, "How good do you want to be?" I didn't ask, "How good of a collegiate athlete do you want to be? I knew he was like Lochte and Seb and a few others before him who wanted more and wanted to be pushed."

Caeleb confirmed Troy's recollections, saying, "I came to Florida to work with Troy. I understood why I was coming to school there. I wanted Troy to make me into something great. I told him, 'I don't want to just be a 50 freestyler. I want you to squeeze out every bit of talent that I have and make me a great athlete.'"

Troy's understanding of the sport and the steps required for Olympic development proved to be an invaluable selling point. "That was one of the easiest buy-ins with Troy. He had the results, you know? He had the swimmers, he's been to the Olympics. He's put people through the Olympics, and he's brought people up from nothing," remembers Caeleb. "He had the track record, which made that buy-in so easy. Some of the other coaches I looked at, they didn't have that track record. They were promising me results that they didn't have history to back up."

Troy's notorious honesty would ultimately help secure the commitment of one of the greatest swimmers in history. True to his reputation and every bit as candid as Caeleb was told he would be, Troy made an essential move in recruiting Caeleb which, in Caeleb's own words, was "not feeding me a bunch of bull crap." Coach Troy's honesty had driven off plenty of recruits in the past, most of whom would have withered under the intensity of the program anyway, but "talking to Troy was a breath of fresh air. Most of my other visits were about making me feel as good as I could be. With Troy, it was basically, "We work really hard here. Don't come if you don't want to. It was essentially like him saying, "You're not tough enough. We can make you into something really good, but it's going to be really hard...but you're probably not up for it. I was like, 'Is this guy for real?' It was the first time I wasn't just being told what I wanted to hear."

As previously mentioned, when college recruiting trips are more of a show than anything else, it can be hard for potential recruits to decipher what's real and true about the program. Those visiting UF, though, seemed to always walk away with a clear picture of what to expect. Some of those recruits left knowing unequivocally they would *not* be attending Florida, and some were stirred to meet the expectations thrown down by the Gator coaching staff. Neither opinion could be made without unflinching honesty from the Gator Head Coach. As Caeleb succinctly put it, "With Troy, even from day one, you know he's shooting straight with you."

Recognizing What Caeleb Needed as a Person and an Athlete

"He is a natural leader, plain and simple," answers Troy when asked about Caeleb's personality. "He has that charisma that attracted people to him. He came into a good dynamic; it was a good culture."

Brad deBorde and Caeleb worked together that first Fall. Recognizing Caeleb was returning to swimming after several months out of the water, and not wanting to completely scare his athlete off, Troy encouraged the two to work together. Together, the sprinters were able to tackle sets that might have seemed out of the ordinary or difficult for either athlete alone. "Quite frankly, we babied him a little bit that first year. We gave him about 3/4ths of that first semester to adjust and never really asked much of him. But, we got lucky because those months out of the water really made him appreciate the sport and appreciate swimming more, recalls Troy of Caeleb's foray into the program. In the semesters following that first year, Troy and the Gators staff would wean Caeleb off the "easy" stuff earlier and earlier.

Adjusting the Traditional Training Plan for a Generational Talent

Coach Troy's long-term vision for Caeleb called for a slow and steady approach to training a generational talent. "That first year, we really trained him like a sprinter," which in Troy parlance means intervals were large, yardage was kept to a relative minimum, and feedback was frequently requested to gauge the athlete's feel. But, the "sprinter life" wouldn't last. By his junior year, Caeleb was entirely removed from the sprint group except for power days, which involved working with resistance, training equipment, and race details.

Caeleb will tell you, "I got compared to Ryan (Lochte), kind of a lot. It took Troy some time to adjust to realize that I'm not the same person as Ryan. Some of the other coaches were the same way. Everyone works differently."

The adjustments to Caeleb's training were designed to be more proactive than reactive. Troy, remembering the earlier years, said, "His Age Group coach at Bolles, Dale Porter, told me, 'If he doesn't have that spark in his eye during training, it ain't gonna happen.' I really took that to heart and we looked for ways to keep him fresh." Adjustments in practice were sometimes uncomfortable for both athlete and coach, though.

As Coach Troy recalls, "there were several times there might have been six different practices going on. One was probably what he *needed*, one was what he *wanted* to do but wasn't right, and we compromised for one of the other middle options that gave him something and gave us something. Sometimes, to his credit, he will take the hardest possible option. He doesn't just do the sprint option, and I think it's a credit to his maturity, but I've seen him more often than not do the option in practice that is hardest because he knows it's what is *right* instead of what is *easy*." That pattern would repeat itself yearly, especially in the first half of any given season, as Caeleb would aim to top the previous limit for his capacity to work.

Caeleb laughingly says, "You know, Troy regularly tells me, 'If you find a shorter, easier way to swim fast...let me know, I probably still won't take that route!' That's just the mindset he has. That's where the communication comes in handy."

That decision-making process and exchange of information between athlete and coach would evolve over time. Now, Caeleb and Troy regularly discuss training options and routes. Both know that neither party will give completely, but they also know that each is committed to doing training the *right* way.

Photo Courtesy of the University Athletic Association

A Personalized Touch: The Coach-Athlete Dynamic

When questioned about whether his relationship with Caeleb is different than his relationships with other world class athletes, Coach Troy paused and stared out the window, contemplating his answer before saying, "Yes and no."

"Yes, in that, I'll always listen to him. I think he's one of the most honest and mature athletes I've ever coached. I listened to previous national champions, I listened to previous Olympic medalists, but I always took their information back and formed my next step around the parameters of their age and were they being honest and where were they fudging it a bit to get by easier."

Caeleb believes, "Everyone works differently. You know, when I worked with Brad deBorde and Coach Steve (Jungbluth), Steve and Troy had to change things that worked for me but didn't work for Brad. I remember telling Steve this year (2019) that the Davis brothers[4] weren't going to respond to things the same way I did. They've got different strengths and different weaknesses."

"I have learned so much from Troy. I would hope it's a beneficial relationship on both ends. I think the main thing is he helps me see the joy in the sport because I could easily get caught up in this being a serious motive for me. He gets it, he knows how

Photo Courtesy of Jack Spitser Photography

I work, and he knows my personality. He knows how far I want to take it. But I hope, on the other end, that he can lean on me for some stuff and see the joy in the sport as well. I've seen that man dance and sing on the deck with the post grad group. He definitely hasn't lost his touch, and that's part of why I'm still working with him."

---

4 Isaac and Will Davis are University of Florida (c/o '22) sprinters and Bolles alum.

"It's crazy because some days we have those practices where he's hungrier to get better than we are. Somedays we're slap dicking around, and he gets on us for it. And he has that passion and joy for the sport to not allow us to cheat ourselves out of our best efforts. I don't want to be coached by a big, old softie because sometimes I need the fire and passion he has to keep us in line."

Swimmer and coach both share the love of improving each season and pushing each other to new heights. "He's clearly still learning and trying new things, which I love and appreciate," says Caeleb. And Troy, to his credit, has adjusted to find new ways to motivate his athletes; the most memorable way in recent history being the infamous "moustache shave" of the 2015-2016 season.

When Coach Troy was asked by the then sophomore at an early season press conference, "How fast would I have to go in the 50 freestyle for you to shave your moustache?" he replied with a chuckle, "Short Course 18.39, Long Course 20.89." It was a playful exchange, but Troy remained true to his word when Caeleb did, in fact, reach and go beyond those goals. The interaction showcases Caeleb's ability to connect with a coach, set outrageous goals, and work hard to achieve said goals for a fun purpose beyond traditional swimming metrics. Coach Troy's understanding of his athlete and what makes him tick, as well as remaining true to his word, solidified the trust and love

of his athletes. Coach's prized whiskers were shaved in the Florida conference room in front of a crowd and gleefully videoed for YouTube. While he was without his trademark facial hair for a few weeks, the connection and trust he gained were definitely worth the funny smirks he had to endure.

Photo Courtesy of the University Athletic Association

CHAPTER ELEVEN
TROY'S LATEST QUADS

Years of prosperity and recognition from the ASCA as the 2010 Coach of the Year helped land Gregg Troy the coveted position of Olympic Head Coach at the 2012 Olympic Games in London. In London, Gregg led the Men's National team to six individual golds, four silvers, three bronzes, and three relay medals (1 silver and 2 gold). Of those sixteen medals, swimmers training directly under Coach Troy back in Gainesville had accounted for six of them.

Elizabeth Beisel, a feisty Rhode Island native and fellow Gator teammate, brought home a bronze medal in the 200-meter backstroke and a silver in the controversial 400 IM final. The performances of Coach Troy's swimmers would further cement his legacy in American coaching. Gregg would be inducted in the American Swimming Coaches Association's Hall of Fame that same year.

Heading up the coaching staff in London was an opportunity Coach Troy attributes largely to the assistance of Associate Head Coach Martyn Wilby's synchronicity and shared value system, as well as Ryan Lochte's success from 2008-2011. The position was the achievement of a lifetime of work and dream come true. The Hall of Fame and successful Olympic Head Coach turned his attention toward Rio and Tokyo.

Photo Courtesy of the University of Florida Athletic Association

Struggles of Co-ed Coaching

Collegiate coaching changed. Not monumentally, nothing had seismically shifted, but the focus had turned and coaches who didn't change with the time struggled.

Social media's constant presence and influence in the lives of teenagers across the world had changed the way coaches were recruiting. Posts on Instagram and Twitter were becoming necessary parts of "selling" the program, school, and city. Per NCAA rules, high school sophomores and juniors were unable to be contacted by coaches first, but they made unofficial visits to collegiate programs and shared about these trips on social media. High schoolers reveled in the attention they received as they posted about their "commitments" to schools many seasons ahead of past classes. As their peers were doing, swimmers often made decisions based on what would garner the most "likes" on social media, rather than what was financially or personally prudent.

On college pool decks across the country, social media was similarly affecting those already in their dream programs. Teams with a stronger social media presence and those who presented a more appealing facade of fun and fast swimming were drawing in the malcontented outliers of other programs. User friendly online transfer portals allowed athletes to transfer from one university to another with more ease than ever before. No longer were university coaches just recruiting high school student-athletes, now they had to recruit their own athletes, season after season to keep them on roster! Coach Troy knew the younger coaches on staff should, could, and would accommodate the shift, so he stuck with the old school ways of communicating directly, putting in the time for face-to-face conversations.

Almost every university felt these struggles in the mid 2010's, but Coach Troy could feel a unique shift specifically within the Florida team, too. Whereas in past years, the Gators had not worn high-tech racing suits, also known as, "suited up," for December meets as a way to develop some mental toughness and grit, each passing year the decision not to suit up was met with more push back and animosity from the athletes. Swimmers were coming into the offices and complaining to assistant coaches (rarely to Gregg directly) about how "unfair it is" that other programs were suiting up regularly and seemingly racing faster for longer periods of time at that mid-season mark. Gregg knew that the amount of work he was putting the team through to prepare for more important end-of-season meets though, was the real reason they didn't look quite as sharp as their competitors come December. But that knowledge wasn't enough to placate a newer generation of athletes who were constantly connected to the goings-on of competitors and friends at other universities. Those same athletes also expected results faster than previous generations; they failed to understand you can't sow what you just planted yesterday.

The coaching staff was also struggling, but for a different reason. The men's and women's teams were each comprised of roughly 30 student-athletes each season. With each of the five coaches on staff seeing each athlete in a different light, Gregg was hearing a total of 300 perspectives on 60 athletes. Even coaches who had coached together for decades and shared coaching philosophies found it difficult to agree on the correct course of action for the majority of the athletes, never mind all 30. Some coaches believed certain swimmers needed more volume; some coaches believed they needed more fun; some coaches could only offer opinions on specific swimmers and were at a loss for the rest. The disconnect among the coaching staff grew as minor snafus began to blossom into major issues.

Unexpected medical tragedies hit some of the Gator women and a lack of scholarship money to replace the afflicted swimmers created holes in meet lineups. Cliques emerged within the larger group, fracturing the cohesion that championship teams need to thrive. The losses of integral teammates were felt at the NCAA Championships that year when the women finished outside of the top 10 at the NCAA Championships in 2016. The 19th place finish was just the beginning of a temporary slump for Florida's women's team. In 2017, they would score not even one point at the same meet. The next year would see a marginal improvement for the Gators with a 35th place finish at NCAAs in 2018. It wasn't until the next year when Jeff Poppell, Troy's Associate Head Coach, would become the sole leader of the Lady Gators and guide the women back to their former excellence. In both 2019 and 2020, the UF women would finish 2nd at the SEC Championships, improving dramatically.

Current Women's Head Coach Jeff Poppell with Kelly Fertel and Sherridon Dressel
Photo Courtesy of the University Athletic Association

Matt DeLancey, Gregg Troy, and Jeff Poppell
Photo courtesy of Kathleen Troy

For coaches leading co-ed programs with multiple coaches on staff, Coach Troy offers this advice:

I still honestly believe split programs are the way to go in today's culture and environment. If you're *forced* to lead a combined program, you have to staff extremely well. You have to allow the staff to work, and at the same time, be extremely conscious that you are moving in one direction. If you start moving in one direction, like the fingers of a fist, you'll be powerful. Once the fingers start to spread and go in different directions, you're in trouble. I think in that dynamic, loyalty and dependability are the two most important factors. Knowledge of the body and sport are good, but those can be taught. You can have a really sharp person, who isn't loyal. Loyalty and dependability are harder, or impossible, to teach. Much like culture, loyalty and dependability are, without a doubt, living organisms and need to be evaluated constantly. Staffs are like marriages, there will be friction, but you need to know how to fight and make up without it breaking the relationship. Don't assume you have loyalty within the staff just because you had loyalty at the start. In a combined program, it has to be very clear who the driver is.

Also, being the head coach of a combined program, or any program for that matter, is being the CEO of a small company. You need to be aware of the non-competitive factors, and you have to be on top of them. I often got caught up between the business side of the sport and the competitive side, and that's when you end up frazzled.

Photo Courtesy of the
University of Florida
Athletic Association

Rio 2016

The group of talented athletes Gregg had under his care in the lead-up to the Rio Olympic Games was a markedly different group than the one he took to London. The 2012 group of Elite Gators was comprised of seasoned veterans: American record holder and Team USA Olympian in '04 and '08, Peter Vanderkaay (a Michigan alum looking for a change in scenery); Big Ten champion Ben Hessen; Ryan Lochte, a world record holder & Olympian in '04 and '08; and 2015 World Champion, Elizabeth Beisel, among others.

The majority of the 2016 group was much younger and far less experienced on the major world stage. A few varsity swimmers were invited to train with Troy's post graduate group prior to the Games and chose to remain; Hilda Luthersdottir (Iceland), Mitch D'Arrigo (Italy), Corey Main (New Zealand) were among them. Others who fell short of making their own country's national teams would join in on the training. Alongside them was Olympic veteran, Arkady Vyatchanin. Arkady, a short course world record holder in the 200 backstroke and 2008 Olympic bronze medalist in the same event, had trained with Coach Troy for a few years. In the lead-up to 2016, he spent time in limbo with the International Olympic Committee and the Serbian Federation. Arkady, a thoughtful and intelligent workhorse, hoped to participate in the 2016 Games as a Serbian, though paperwork and bureaucratic red tape would ultimately sideline his dreams.

"2012 was led by guys and girls with enormously helpful experience at the world level, and the leadership came *from* that group. They questioned the coaching and instruction more, but in a good way. They wanted to know why things were being done, but once they knew, it was like a rolling rock. The 2016 group was led by less experienced, younger talent who were willing to do pretty much anything that was thrown at them, but *I* supplied the leadership," said Troy.

Per Coach Troy, a huge benefit of having the professional group training for Rio in the same facilities where the collegiate group trained was "that you can have an especially good set one day with the postgrad group and then those other collegiate guys know when they come in the next day that they're looking at a little bit of a higher standard."

Caeleb recalls, "Having other guys around me with the same goals really drove me. Jan, Mark, and I would compete in practice. I hate losing, especially to Jan and Mark. I'm not a sore loser, but there are people I hate losing to more than others and Mark, Jan and Lochte are at the top of the list." With his teammates pushing him to new heights in practice, forcing him to confront potential weaknesses, Caeleb flourished.

In Rio, Caeleb Dressel would win his first gold medal in the 4x100-meter freestyle relay. He swam in the final of the event, leading off the first leg. His 48.10 split was the second fastest opening leg, leaving Team USA poised to take over the lead as Michael Phelps, Ryan Held, and Nathan Adrian still to follow. The Americans would finish the relay with a time of 3:09.92.

Caeleb would swim even faster in the 100-meter freestyle individually, finishing sixth in the A final of the event with a time of 48.02. Dressel would also swim in the morning prelim heats of the 4x100-meter medley relay, earning his second gold medal as the USA finished first in the championship finals. He recorded a freestyle split of 47.74 in the prelim heats.

Photo Courtesy of Jack
Spitser Photography

Elizabeth Beisel would go on to finish 6th in the 400-meter Individual Medley with a time of 4:36.38. Though the 6th place finish was not quite an ideal ending for the elite Olympian, if there was a dip in her positivity, it went undetected by her teammates. Elizabeth would play a pivotal role as an influential and demonstrative team captain, backing teammates and helping guide younger athletes and seasoned veterans to 33 overall medals and 16 gold medals.

The Latest Cycle: The Road to Tokyo

It's common to hear coaches spouting off complaints about the recent generation of kids, saying things like, "These kids won't train like athletes used to back in the day." Coaches with 20 or 30 years of experience under their belts will blame poor meet performances on generational stereotypes perpetuated by online articles written by Boomer and Gen X authors.

Coach Troy dislikes hearing those digs at up-and-coming swimmers and will tell you, "I think that's just wrong. They will work just as hard, if not harder, than anyone else. The difference is they have way more information and knowledge at their fingertips, so they want to have what they are doing explained to them. They want to know you know what you're talking about and what you're asking from them."

While swimming has seen changes over the decades, at its core, the sport is still the same. A coach, and the athletes working with said coach, need to agree on common goals, on what kind of work needs to be done to close the gap between "where we are now" and "where we want to go." Then, the coach and swimmer need to understand and trust each other enough to allow both sides to challenge each other appropriately.

Following Ryan Lochte's venture to Charlotte and eventually to Los Angeles, the Olympic veteran realized a component was missing in his training. "Going to Charlotte was probably the only regret I have in my swimming career instead of just taking a year-long break," realized Ryan. While Team Elite's Coach Marsh offered a new and nuanced coaching style, Ryan came to the conclusion that the reason he was so good for so long was because of his commitment to the basics and to the *hard, challenging work* that he had done with

Coach Troy for so long. "Once my son was born, I realized I wanted to give this another shot. And if I'm going to give this another shot, I gotta do this right. If I needed to do it right, I needed to go full throttle and go back to where it started. I knew the only person and coach who knew what I needed as a person and an athlete was Troy."

With Coach Troy's retirement from NCAA coaching and his return to club coaching, Caeleb, Ryan, and the rest of the Gator Swim Club's High-Performance group are training under the coach they trust. Though young, these swimmers still possess the good, old-fashioned work ethic of yore, they just have a more inquisitive spirit that needs tending. Coach Troy has adapted to best develop this fresh crop of athletes. The work ethic of this young generation is not what has to change, rather, a coach's willingness to listen to his athletes and spend a little more time explaining the process. Using information in the form of online advice from faraway colleagues, bringing in other experts from USA Swimming, or analyzing video feedback from sport scientists like those at the Race Club are just a few tactics that Troy uses to ensure his athletes know they are getting the best possible information from their trusted coach.

Coach Troy still doesn't like texting, and his emails are so brief they sometimes read like telegrams, but that's done on purpose. Coach knows athletes hide behind the comfort that phones, texting, and email afford. He enjoys face-to-face conversation and the information one gains through those direct interactions. It's through those personal conversations that Coach gathers how his athletes are *really* feeling, even if they answer with the default go-to, "Fine."

With the change in practice style and philosophical focus, that communication and understanding of his athletes' needs has never in his career been more important. While the group dynamic will never be an obsolete issue for Coach Troy, gone are the days of worrying about more than 50 swimmers at a time. Without having to worry about the group as a massive whole, Coach is better able to focus on the individual needs of each athlete and how to best adjust them. Just as Donna S* needed a more individualized practice plan back in the late 90s, the young men and women globe-trotting to international meets as professional athletes need programs designed specifically for them.

What's Changed? What's the Same?

When asked about what has remained constant and what has changed in coaching over the years, Coach Troy pauses to think before answering, "Constants? Working 'hard,' if you want to call it that, or 'challenging work' works. Intensity is key. Goal setting and direction are important: knowing where you're going is vital. And, there's more to it than just swimming."

He goes on, "Changes in my coaching? There's more maturity on my part in knowing that there are more than one or two ways to get something done and get the same product. Oddly enough, some of the same things that remained the same for me are also what changed, like understanding that there's more than just swimming. Having raised three competitive sons myself, and having seen their development through sports, I know coaches played a huge part in their development. At Bolles, I was around a few good coaches. But at UF, I was surrounded by amazing coaches. The constant bombardment of ideas and methods just reinforced the idea that there's more to the world than swimming and what we're doing extends beyond the pool. That change took me time, but I definitely absorbed it over my time at UF."

Caroline Burckle, a 2008 U.S. Olympic medalist, Florida Gator alumnus, and once NCAA record holder in the 500 Freestyle, talked about adjustments that were required for her training in the UF program under Coach Troy and Coach Wilby. The process of Coach Troy learning how to adjust to an athlete's needs came up in a conversation between Caroline and Brett Hawke on Coach Hawke's podcast, "Inside with Brett Hawke." Caroline spoke about her specific needs as an athlete, saying, "I struggled to explain myself. I was not your typical swimmer who needed to know their splits or train like other people would train for the 500. I just didn't. I kept trying to explain that I don't do well with numbers or splits and that we needed to find another way to communicate, whether it was about my tempo or with imagery. That took my entire sophomore year of college. We had a huge meeting finally and we talked about what works for me, what doesn't, what fears I have, why I feel that way, and it all amounted to I needed to find a different way to assess my races to perform. After that meeting and from that day on, it was lights out because he no longer gave me my splits. No matter what we did in practice, I never heard my times. I only heard my tempo and there would be some days when he would just look at me and he could just feel my needs. Some days, he would just tell me, 'I want you to get in and do a thousand yards and get out.' It wasn't liked by my teammates, but it worked." Coach Troy and the UF staff learned, in a different way, from Caroline and adjusted their coaching to better fit the individual needs of their athletes. That lesson, which Coach Troy kept refining every year, would play into preparations for Tokyo enormously.

Three Practice Cycle

Leaving behind the University of Florida varsity practice schedule forced Coach Troy to change the way he planned and executed training for the swimmers still under his care. By creating the "High-Performance International Group" within Gator Swim Club, the local club team operating out of the O'Connell Center, Coach Troy was able to bring elite athletes under one banner with minimal disruptions. Swimmers from around the world had contacted Gregg about the possibility of joining his training group. True Sweetser, a USA National Champion in the 1500 Freestyle and once National team member, returned from college at Stanford, where he took a redshirt year to prepare for the U.S. Olympic trials. Canadian gold medalist, Penny Oleksiak, made a change to her training style and preparation by joining the GSC squad at one point, too. The group was made up of some of the best swimmers in the world with a few vying for spots on their respective national teams. With just over 18 months until most 2020 Olympic trials would begin, there wasn't any time to waste.

Practice hours for the new training group shifted and changed, as did the focus points of training. When he was overseeing the development of the entire Men's and Women's varsity teams at UF, Coach Troy worried constantly and concerned himself with the fitness levels of incoming freshmen and upperclassmen returning from training at home over the summer. Enormous chunks of each season were spent ensuring the aerobic training levels and the capacities of each athlete were maximized. Working with 23 to 35-year-old mature, elite level, professional athletes though, would not necessarily require the same devotion to building endurance. The smaller group with more experienced swimmers afforded Coach Troy the chance to create a group dynamic that highlighted each swimmer's individual needs. Purposeful speed training and highly specific workouts would become staples of the pro group.

One major shift in practice management came in the form of a three-practice cycle run three times within a week. "After watching other small 'professional' and 'elite' groups, I was honestly afraid of being *too specialized* and missing out on the group element of what we were going to do." Coach Troy explains, "The idea became to run three practices. The first was, for lack of a better term, an 'old school' group workout. No complaining—just do what's asked. The last was more individual and largely what they thought they needed. The athletes came to me with ideas and we adjusted and fine-tuned thoughts until we got some really good stuff going. The middle workout was a combination of old school and their perceived needs. Now, it wasn't all perfect. We lost one or two athletes who wouldn't conform to the first old school workout, but that's alright. I feel like we're running what we need right now."

Similarities Between Caeleb and Ryan

"You know, both guys are pretty social animals," muses Troy. "They're busy outside of the pool and engaged in a lot of things. You've got to work to keep them on track and make sure they're really engaged in what they're doing with training. They're also competitors like no one has ever seen," Troy notes on shared similarities of the two Gator greats.

"Coaches need to understand how to use someone's competitiveness to their advantage. It's something that they have to use in practice often enough it's helping them improve, they have to race often enough to enjoy the competition outside of practice, and then they can't do either of those things too much or you just deaden them to the positive effects they feel from it. It's a real balancing act."

Feedback is another area in which both Olympians are compatible with Coach Troy. "Both guys (Caeleb and Ryan) are truly honest. They do the work the way I ask it to be done. They commit themselves to the sessions we plan and then when they tell me how they're feeling or if they're sluggish, I know I can trust it. The feedback they give is real."

"Caeleb and I were talking the other day," Troy says, "and he told me, 'This year, I don't want to feel as run down as I did last year from all that we did.' Mind you, he racked in the gold medals at World Champs, so I told him I thought that was part of the reason he did so well. After some convincing he agreed we probably need the status quo, but he followed up by asking, 'When we get closer to Tokyo, you're going to listen to me and what my body is feeling, right?' And the answer from my end has to be *YES*. When someone commits to every practice like he does and has accomplished what he has, I have to listen to him as his coach. It'll create some friction when he tells me he thinks he needs to back off and I don't agree, but that friction will make me a better coach and will help me realize what the athletes really need."

Caeleb agrees, "It's nice to have someone like that on my team. Someone who isn't complacent, someone who is not afraid to yell at you and tell you how it is and at the end of the day, we know we're still going to be really good friends. But, I mean, he yells at me. And I'll probably yell back. We've had extremely heated moments, but at the end of the day, he's still my coach and my friend and I want a guy who's not going to get soft with me. And that is Troy."

Managing a new father, a new professional, the pressures of travel and business, and the ISL

The road to Tokyo has by no means been a smooth asphalt highway for anyone in the Gator pro group. When asked about what the adjustments are like for Lochte and Dressel, Coach Troy just laughed. "Because of the duties of fatherhood like doctor's trips and ultrasound videos, Lochte still misses occasional practice, but it's a new kind of adjustment for me!" acknowledges Troy, "I'm used to his wild nights as a college athlete, but this is a new type of adjustment."

Knowing when to push thirty-four-year-old Lochte and knowing when to recognize honest physical breakdown has become vital to Coach Troy's planning and daily practice modifications. "He is spectacular when he's great, but when he falls off because of weights or late nights or whatever the reason, he *really* falls off in practice. Knowing how to adjust based on that has become necessary." Age does funny things.

Photo Courtesy of Jack Spitser Photography

As Ryan recalls, "In the beginning, he thought I was still my old self. I'd 'go to the well' and all that stuff, but I'd be dying a lot quicker."

The lack of sleep and recovery at night, coupled with energized children who wanted to play and be active, made for an interesting reintroduction for the Gator great back to the world of elite training. "I was a lot older; I wasn't getting as much recovery as I used to, and I didn't have the luxury of taking naps and things like that. All that considered, it was hard for me to want to get up and go to practice with a great attitude sometimes. It was just so much harder." Coach Troy came around though and, after toying with different variations of workouts and training cycles, he came to realize Ryan wasn't the same athlete he used to be and required a different workload and delivery system. Days off and adjusted warm downs have become regularly used tools. Coach Troy works with Ryan to create the most effective and efficient training schedule.

"I still have the same mentality and I'm still willing to 'go to the well,' but it happens quicker and it's a shorter burst of speed. With that, Coach has changed certain aspects. I might do half the number of 400s the rest of the group does, but I do them faster than I otherwise would and then I end up doing way more warmdown than anyone else," says Ryan. "He's understanding and I communicate with him nonstop to keep that relationship of listening going."

Caeleb, on the other hand, is going through slightly more familiar territory for Coach Troy. Becoming a new professional athlete in the ISL (International Swimming League) Caeleb uses advertising opportunities through Speedo to make a living as a professional swimmer. His busier schedule requires Coach Troy to make adjustments to training in order to work around weekend travel for photo shoots and more. Coach Troy collaborates with Caeleb's agent but isn't shy about expressing his worries when appearances and photoshoots get in the way of truly valuable training, but also acknowledges those same professional demands are what allow Caeleb to swim for a living.

Fluid training plans and accommodations are necessary for continuous, purposeful training, but as Dylan Carter, a Trinidad Olympian has commented, "Traveling for the ISL and for international meets is exhausting and it definitely takes away from training."

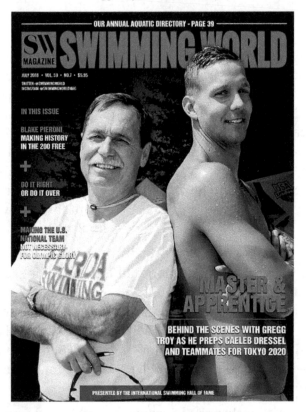

Discussing the differences between collegiate training and his new professional group, Caeleb explains, "We're all grown men at this point. If someone's getting soft and they don't show up to practice, there's not forty other guys to yell at him. But, there are some instances where you can get soft on yourself as a professional and with travel, appearances, and everything like that, it's a whole different ball game. There's a lot more travel and logistics involved, but it comes back on me and how honest I'm being with myself and with Troy. You have got to hold yourself accountable, even more so in a post-grad group than in college, because you don't have those guys there to back you up or call you out. It's harder with a smaller group and when people notice that you're gone. It all comes back to honesty though. I know he's had practice with Ryan, but Troy's great about keeping the group hungry and motivated around our schedules." Commitment and self-discipline at the professional level are vital, though many tend to take a step back and do less because of the feeling of having "made it."

Photo courtesy of Caeleb Dressel

As Troy considers Caeleb's foray into professional swimming and training around marketing requirements he says, "After learning through trial and error with Ryan, and knowing Caeleb's maturity, I usually send Caeleb with a workout plan about 80 percent of the time when he's gone on photoshoots and whatnot. The other 20 percent of the time, if he's been good at home, I'll send vague instructions like, "Do 3,000 yards worth of heart rate work," and I trust he's going to get it done." That trust, though, was hard earned, and took years of relentless training done back to back to back to garner.

Photo Courtesy of Jack Spitser Photography

In an interview with Ryan, I relay to him Coach Troy's thoughts on Caeleb's development and, ever competitive, Ryan is quick to let me know, "I'm doing better than I've ever done with the travel workouts and whatnot. I'm taking way more accountability for myself, and if Troy gives me practices, I'm actually going to the pool and doing them instead of procrastinating like I used to." It's scary to think about how good Ryan will be if he's just *now* beginning to take travel practices seriously...

When You're the Best, What's "Enough?" What's "Too Much?"

At one point or another, every athlete in the history of sports has wondered if their coach has lost their mind. Every athlete hits a breaking point at some moment in training, when they question the validity of what's being asked of them. Some coaches use faster intervals, some add resistance, some add yardage, and others get truly creative in the ways they challenge their athletes.

With over 45 years of coaching experience, and more than 60 Olympians on his resumé; with international medals, and numerous American, U.S. Open, and World records attributed to his coaching, it's hard to believe anyone would still question Coach Troy's methods or practice demands. Perhaps, the one person with grounds to question him would be the person most familiar with his methods, and the one of the fastest humans to ever swim, Caeleb Dressel.

It's early February, 18 months away from the 2021 Games in Tokyo, when I call Coach Troy for a short interview.*5 We start by talking about how our respective practices went that Saturday when Coach tells me an interesting story from the week.

"Jackson, I decided last weekend that this week we were going to go four rounds of 30x100s throughout the week. Monday, we came in and went a variety of 30x100s backstroke; pretty aerobic. Tuesday, we did a few rounds of breaststroke ones. I got creative Wednesday and came back to hit them with a strong set of 30x100s freestyle on Thursday, knowing I wanted to do butterfly for our Flyday Friday. But, by the time yesterday rolled around, we just looked too rough to get them done well. So, I figured I'd save them for this morning. About ten 100s into the set this morning, I knew it wasn't right physically. Mentally, maybe there was something for them to pull from the set, but physically, I wasn't doing anyone any favors."

He went on, "So, I had to make some quick decisions. I knew doing trash technique wasn't going to help, so I offered Caeleb the option of going just six blast cycles of butterfly off each wall before shutting it down. He wasn't too happy with me, or the idea of a fourth

---

5 This conversation happened months before COVID-19 changed 2020 Olympic plans. The practice was planned as if Tokyo was only 6 months away.

round of 30x100s, or the idea of doing these fly...so he pretty much gave me a big eye roll and kept plugging away at it. Since I'd offered him that option, I felt I had to offer the other guys and gals that option, too. They also gave me eye rolls. After a few more, I offered a concession, again. This time I told them they could wear whatever gear they wanted: fins, paddles, snorkel, whatever they needed to make the strokes worthwhile. I'm pretty sure at that point I got a few middle fingers when I wasn't looking. But I'll give it to them, everyone finished all 30 going full fly. It got ugly stroke-wise toward the end, but there's no doubt they're mentally a tough group."

There I was, worrying about whether or not I was pushing my Futures qualifiers too hard that morning and the reigning world champion was grinding out 30x100s for the fourth time in a week! Coach Troy continued, "So Caeleb got out and was pretty annoyed with me. He told me flat out, 'I'm too old to be doing this shit.' And, maybe he's right. But what I told him, and what I believe, is, 'No one's ever done what you've done and if we're going to keep it that way, you're going to keep doing what's worked. So, until it's wrong, it's the right thing to do.'"

I chuckle into the phone and Coach Troy finishes our conversation with one more thought. "I told you that story about pushing too hard the one season at Bolles. Now, I still relive that season in my mind once in a while, but without that season… I wouldn't have known if today was crossing the line or not. I'm pretty sure this week I took Caeleb *to* the line. But we didn't cross it; and that's because I learned the hard way. I firmly believe you've got to push athletes right to the edge. They have to be pushed so hard that you go home wondering and worried if they are going to come back the next day."

I hung up the phone and counted the days until the Tokyo Games. I smiled to myself and couldn't help but think, *if, at six months out, Coach Troy is taking the best in the world to what he considers the line repeatedly, I feel sorry for the rest of the world's swimmers who have to compete against him.*

CHAPTER TWELVE

THE FUTURE

Photo Courtesy of the University Athletic Association

Family and Reflection

With the hectic days of being the Head Coach of the University of Florida's varsity teams behind him, Coach Troy's pace has slowed considerably. Simple pleasures like taking his dog for a longer walk around the Haile Plantation neighborhoods in west Gainesville, or escaping to and from Cedar Key, allow for time to think and reflect.

Cedar Key, a quiet coastal town on the west coast of Florida, is a favorite fishing and relaxation spot for the Troy family. Just a short drive from Gainesville, Cedar Key has become a frequently visited getaway for Gregg and his wife, Kathleen.

Coach Troy fishing in Cedar Key
Photo courtesy of Kathleen Troy

As they travel west on State Road 24, the Troys listen to "The Roadhouse," a Sirius XM radio station for classic country—only Cash, Hank, Willie, and Waylon for Gregg; none of the new stuff. It's not surprising that the man who preaches consistency, character, and honest work appreciates listening to music that is considered the heartbeat of the working class. Greg and Kathleen make idle chatter as they relish the drive out of town. Once in Cedar Key, Gregg is able to disconnect and enjoy his time with his thoughts and memories.

Six years ago, Coach Troy lost a dear friend and colleague, Donnie Craine, in a tragic boating accident. Donnie, the University of Florida's head diving coach was a jack of all trades, and an avid Cedar Key fisherman. It's there that Coach Troy gets to spend quiet mornings on the water catching up with Donnie in spirit.

Even when Troy is physically away from the pool, in one form or another swimming always finds him. Mentees often call Troy even on his weekends off to chat. He is always game to take time for these calls, even on drives to Cedar Key or idle moments at sea while waiting for the fish to bite. Coaches, like Sarasota Sharks head coach and USA National team Coach Brent Arckey, once a volunteer assistant for Coach Troy, regularly calls his mentor to chat about training and the goings on in the club swimming world. Coach Troy's brain, a whirlwind of swimming knowledge, is forced to slow down a bit now as he also shares those car rides and walks with his dog and with his wife, Kathleen.

Troy's willingness to rattle off about swimming at the drop of a hat is commonplace to Kathleen Troy. A former swimmer, Kathleen understands the ins and outs of the sport. She's been on a pool deck in some capacity since high school, and never far from Coach Troy. As Greg Burgess recalls, "Mrs. Troy was synonymous with Bolles swimming. She was always on deck helping out in a lot of ways, whether it was teaching swim lessons or just doing what was needed. I can't remember times when she wasn't there by Gregg's side."

You'd be hard pressed to find a former swimmer at Bolles or the University of Florida who cannot remember Mrs. Troy teaching swim lessons or helping coaches around the deck. An integral part of each of Coach Troy's endeavors, Mrs. Troy has remained by Gregg's side to see the amazing results he's helped bring about. Coach Troy, in our interviews, insisted that I make sure I am clear: he *could not* have achieved anything without her support and love.

Gregg and Kathleen, on their wedding day (left) and vacationing (right)

Gregg may have made a good Lone Ranger as a kid...

But it's Kathleen who completes him
Photos courtesy of Kathleen Troy

The newfound flexibility in Coach Troy's schedule allows for another welcome change to his life—additional time spent with his sons, Patrick, Geoffrey, and Ryan Troy. Coaching at such a high level for so long meant making sacrifices, often in the form of missing his sons' Saturday morning youth sports games and first days of school to be at meets or practice with his team. Now, he is making up for lost years, spending time traveling to be with his boys and being part of their lives.

Gregg and his son, Ryan
Photo courtesy of Kathleen Troy

His now grown sons realize the important role that swimming played in their father's life, and they know how impactful he was and still is for the many athletes he's trained. Early in 2020, Coach Troy attempted to throw out over 35 binders filled with decades worth of logbooks and workouts that had been collecting dust in a closet. When Gregg's oldest son caught him hauling the binders out with the trash, he immediately stopped his father and convinced him to keep the mementos. The Troy family knows just how important swimming is to them.

Coach Terry Maul, the former head coach for the USA National and Junior National teams, and head coach of the Florida State

University Seminole swimming and diving teams from 1975-1993, is a close friend of Gregg's. "I think some people don't know it, but Gregg is a true patriot." With Gregg's father a World War II veteran and his middle son, Geoffrey, a distinguished Major in the U.S. Marine Corps, Gregg takes pride in his family's commitment to the country he so proudly represents in the international sporting world.

Troy Family
Photo courtesy of Kathleen Troy

"While what Geoffrey does is dangerous," says Coach Troy, "I appreciate that we have people in this country who are willing and able to act on behalf of the entire country. I'm even more proud that someone in my own family is willing to do so." Speaking about his son, a pilot who went through an American service academy and "did it the hard way," Coach Troy notes that Geoffrey is humble, almost to a fault. "He didn't really explain how important his promotion to Major was, and it wasn't until a family friend explained it that we really grasped as a family how important his advancement had been."

Gregg, Kathleen, and Patrick
Photo courtesy of Kathleen Troy

The oldest Troy son, Patrick, is a recently promoted junior CEO of a multi-million-dollar company. He moved up the ranks by maintaining a sense of humility and respect for his elders, while not being afraid to speak his mind. Patrick has applied lessons and value structures learned from growing up as a middle-distance track athlete and a son of Gregg Troy to his own professional life. After being promoted, Patrick called his father and commented, "I got this hefty raise and nice title, but man, the work increased exponentially."

Coach Troy, always thinking in swimming terms, automatically relates his son's comments to the current state of professional swimming. "These 'pros' think because they've suddenly made it in the ISL, they now get to do less and swim just as fast. NO! In the real world, and in swimming, once you reach a new point, you may have a fancy title or nice raise but you're going to pay either with time or commitment. There's no doing *less* just because you move up a level."

Coach Troy's youngest, Ryan, was raised with the same values as his brothers, but took slightly more time to figure out his passion and intended direction. After obtaining his degree in Outdoor Education, Ryan worked hard and took his Captain's licensing courses with the former UF Diving coach, Coach Craine. He is now a prominent freshwater and saltwater fly fishing guide working in both southeastern Idaho (where his home is) and the Florida Keys.

Because of his work and the guests he entertains and helps, Coach Troy believes his youngest son to be the most sensitive and patient of the three.

When I asked Coach Troy about his sons, as we sat in a diner off the interstate in Gainesville, he said, "Of all three, I'm proud they have become successful in their individual endeavors and are happy with what they do." This father's pride in his sons' fierce independence and commitment to family values was plainly evident by our conversation's end.

Quick Responses on a Variety of Subjects:

The following were assorted questions I asked Coach Troy, Caeleb, and Ryan. The answers were vitally important but didn't quite fit into any specific chapter. Their quick answers are meant to be easily referenced if needed.

What do young coaches who are just starting out need to know?

Coach Troy: I believe coaches who are just starting out need to understand this job is a passion. I see it, and I hear about it all the time now. I recently talked to a good friend who runs a coaches' clinic on the west coast of Florida in late September. I asked about the attendance this past year and my friend told me it was a lot of older coaches, but not many young guys and girls. Millennials don't seem to want to give up their weekends or spend vacation days on work trips. But I think that's backward. If what you're doing every day isn't your passion, especially when it comes to working with kids, everyone's going to know you don't really want to be there.

I firmly believe the elective classes in teaching that my father made me take were the classes that influenced my coaching most directly. Coaches today who don't want to teach and aren't passionate about working with children will never accomplish as much as those who do. And understanding the kids you work with is the next step to that. Everyone wants to tell you that Gen Z kids won't work or can't pay attention; no, coaches just need to get better at explaining what they want and need to do a better job selling their own programs to better informed kids. These kids are willing to do everything the kids in the '80s were willing to do; in fact, they want to do it and then share their experience online with all their friends!

I think having support from your family and surrounding coaches is also vital. I wouldn't have been successful without my wife and family supporting me and tolerating the job's requirements. Their support was the bedrock to any success I had.

I wouldn't have been successful without the Athletic Directors who backed me. I wouldn't have been successful without assistant coaches who filled in the gaps I left and acted as sounding boards for the ideas I'd bring in.

Lastly, I think the last tool a coach needs on deck is his or her stopwatch. There are so many other tools that need to be developed before learning how to give splits and what the splits mean. Passion for what you're doing, and teaching skills definitely needs to come first.

*Author's note: As Shelley Burgess and Beth Houf note in their book, *Lead Like a Pirate*: "Teaching is incredibly complex! It involves classroom management, engagement techniques, depth of content knowledge, precise use of effective instructional practices, wise use of resources, an understanding of assessment and how to use it, long-term planning, and short-term adjustments. It involves knowing the unique learning needs of each child in the classroom and developing strategies to reach them and help them thrive. It involves grit, determination, persistence, flexibility, an element of fun, and a whole lot of heart!" That sounds identical to effective coaching! If one of the greatest coaches in swimming history espousing the importance of teaching skills doesn't convince you to work on those skills, you will continue to be hampered as a coach.

What is necessary for future coaches to continue to help athletes produce world-leading times?

Coach Troy: Don't be afraid to push the envelope. Coaches today are too afraid to push athletes to the edge for fear of what their parents will say, their friends will report, or what administrators will do. Every time you want something special from your kids in practice, if you don't leave wondering, "Will they come back tomorrow?" you didn't push them hard enough. It's challenging and you'll worry yourself sick, but it's the only way to produce world-leading swims.

Gregg at a Team USA press conference, 2012
Photo courtesy of Kathleen Troy

List of coaches you believe today's up-and-coming coaches should know and study from?

Coach Troy: Pete Malone is one, for sure. Pete worked for the Kansas City Blazers. He was always very articulate and very technical about what he did. He could give you great information in a way you understood. Smart, smart guy.

Doc Councilman and his book, *The Science of Swimming,* is the essential starting point for all coaches. Everyone needs to read it.

Ernie Maglischo is a fantastic coach/ scientist and is an honest combination of both. He knows the science but can relate it to everyday coaching.

Bill Sweetenham, he's worked with most Commonwealth programs and is a fantastic source of knowledge.

On the other end, there's Eddie Reese, Mark Schubert, Richard Quick, and David Marsh. All of those guys are special when it comes to the art of coaching. David, although a rival for so long, has a special way of communicating certain ideas and connecting with athletes.

Finally, I think younger coaches need to connect with peers in their own age group. Reading on past coaches is great but connecting with those your own age can help connect dots quicker and help you understand the current vision easier.

What is/are the next technological tool (s) that coaches should be using in practice regularly?

Coach Troy: There are actually a few that I think coaches need to use every day. I am amazed when I watch other practices because I watch coaches give feedback and make stroke corrections with nothing but words or occasionally a demonstration. I can recall the days when we had to spend $100 at H. H. Gregg on handheld camcorders so we could video swimmers, pull them out of the water, plug the camera into a TV on deck, just to show them a stroke deficiency.

Now, every single coach I know has a fancy iPhone in their pocket with a better camera than I ever bought. It takes you less than five seconds to pull up your video camera function, and yet, very rarely do I see that utilized. We know that Gen Z kids learn better through visual learning, just look at how much time they spend learning basic tasks from YouTube tutorials. Coaches need to learn how to efficiently film an athlete doing something wrong, pull them out at an appropriate time within the workout, allow them to make the change after seeing a ten second clip, and then—and this is the important part—circle back to give feedback. It's just counterintuitive to keep teaching the way we *had to* before cameras and video was so readily accessible.

The other piece of technology that I know can be used ever more frequently and more efficiently than I use it, is an innovation from one of my first swimmers, David McCagg. Caeleb and Ryan have been using the GMX7-X1 Pro training tool pretty consistently. As a sport, we've been using the same couple of forms of resistance for forever. We use buckets, pulleys, parachutes, sponges, whatever. David was probably one of the first guys doing buckets with Randy Reese back in the early '80s, but he's come up with this new innovation that is pretty minimal and not too invasive, and it's way more consistent and replicable than chutes and bulky buckets with weight.

The last isn't technology, but I'm going to say it anyway—courses on psychology and education. I think it should be mandatory that all coaches have teaching certificates. Kinesiology and biomechanics are great, but if you can't communicate those ideas to your athletes, the ideas are useless… It used to be that teachers supplemented with coaching or vice versa, so the skills were shared. But now, coaches don't want to work on basic classroom management skills, even though we're teachers in an aquatic setting!

What are the pros and cons for more swimmers participating in the ISL?

Coach Troy:

Pros:

- It provides quality, brief competition. You're not there for hours getting beat up. When you're older, that's key.

- It has potential to be more fan and TV-friendly. I'm not just talking about moms and dads but about the swammers who want to be a part of swimming life still. Part of the reason the stands are packed at most football games is because guys who played the sport 10, 20, 30 years ago get to relive their glory days. Right now, we have swimmers leave the sport and never come back to watch or re-engage. That's poor marketing on our leaders' part. Swimming may have a more consistent venue for that with the ISL. We have to encourage that.

- It adds to the twinkle in the athletes' eyes, I was talking about earlier. It was laborious to get Caeleb to do the necessary work in the Fall of 2019 until after the first ISL meet. After we came back from that though, the training just took off to a new level. I think coaches are seeing that all over.

Cons:

- Competitions that are too frequent. I'm actually not willing to call it a pro or con because I don't know for certain where the sport is going in the future. But the ISL could de-emphasize the Olympic-type swimming and the Olympic ideal, but that could be a good thing. Maybe the Olympics will go away anyway.

Somewhere between both:

- The novelty of it. Does that wear off after a few years? Everyone is currently all amped up about it, but we need to refine the dynamic.

Favorite IM set?

4x50 Fly LCM @ 1:00

SCY @ :45

3x400 Free IM

LCM @ 6:00, SCY @ 5:00

Easy 3x100 @ 1:30

Repeat, but drop on the 400 Free IM each time.

Sometimes the last set of 50s are smooth free but then normal 400 IMs. I have played with several intervals. The set came in some form from Chuck Batchelor.

-I like it because it is a good indicator of conditioning and predictor of performance.

Favorites speed set?

8x50

4 @ 2:00

2 @ 1:30

2 @ :50 SCY, 1:00 LCM

*can be done several times, usually 2-3 rounds

LCM - It's more of a 200 oriented set.

SCY - It's real speed for coming home.

* All done from dive

All all-out, no descend

- Compliments of Australian coaches by way of Richard Quick

Favorite team set?

Broken 200s

SCY

75 Fast @ :40

50 EZ @1:00

50 Fast @ :30

50 EZ @1:00

50 Fast @ :25

50 EZ @1:00

25 Fast @ :10

200 Easy with great technique

It teaches race speeds and is just fun to do. Athletes like it and it is great race conditioning. It really gets tough where the race is tough. It's a pretty good way to motivate athletes as there is good contact time on the easy portions.

*Repeat up to 6 times

From: Tim Hill in the '80s

What do athletes need to continue doing to be successful?

Ryan: For me, just knowing swimming, you can't be satisfied. You can't be satisfied with what you get. You have to always be hungry and you have to want more. That is the only way. Because if you want more, you're going to set goals higher and you're going to wake up every day wanting to work to achieve something greater than you've already done. People are getting complacent, like, "Oh, I broke a world record." or, "Oh, I won a gold medal, so I don't really need to do much." *NO.* You have to find ways to make yourself better because people are finding ways to catch you.

Photo Courtesy of Jack Spitser Photography

Caeleb: You can't get complacent. You have to stay hungry. I think Ryan said it best to me; whenever he's the top time in the world, you can never see yourself as that. I learned that from him. You can never see yourself as the fastest in the world. If you do, someone's going to be passing you. It just comes back to complacency. Complacency kills. Maybe you are at the top of your game but put a target on your own back and chase to be faster than the old version of yourself. 2019 for me was a good year, but I'm not satisfied with it. I feel like it could have been so much better, so I'm looking for ways to get better, and that's whether I'm coming off a good swim or a bad swim. So, not being complacent is the biggest thing.

How much of success is determined by your coach's abilities/ knowledge and how much is determined by the athlete's personality?

Ryan: It's not one or the other. It's not a one-man show. It's a group effort; it's a family. You have to believe in your coach and your coach has to believe in you. You can't lie; you have to be honest. You have to communicate; it takes effort.

Caeleb: It's 50/50. It's exactly down the middle. I would not be able to make it as far as I have if it was just me on my own. I need those crazy, "What the heck?" kind of practices from Troy if I want to get to those crazy, "What the heck?" kind of goals I have for myself. It goes hand in hand. I let my personality come through in practice. Practices are fun. We like to make fun of each other, we like to throw some heat and throw some shade; that's how I work. Just let those personalities come through more each year and let those emotions out at practice.

If I'm a robot and just do everything Troy says, it's only going to get me so far. If I don't listen to Coach Troy, it's only going to get me so far. I need both. I need that personality to shine through at practice, but I also need Troy to give us those magical sets to get to work on.

Difference(s) in training, motivation, etc., between CT and Coach Marsh at the professional level?

Ryan: Both have their specific skill sets. Coach Marsh definitely broke down the strokes into the smallest possible components. He would talk about moving your fingertips an inch this way or that way and it was really, really detailed. For a lot of people, they wanted and needed that. Troy is a little more of a blunt object, but he knows the stroke details I need and communicates them in a way that I get and can adjust from.

Gregg and Ryan Lochte at the Golden Goggles Awards, 2008
Photo courtesy of Kathleen Troy

Biggest worry moving forward if Coach Troy isn't coaching you?

Caeleb: I don't have a worry. I came to UF because of Troy, but this is my home now. Nesty, Steve, and my strength coach, Matt, are all here. It wasn't just Troy that got me to where I'm at; it was the athletic department as a whole, it was Matt, my strength coach, Steve, Nesty, Coach Wilby, and Leah. It's all these guys. It's never just one person. So, I don't see myself leaving UF at all. I have my guys here, I have my routine here, and this is where I've built myself up.

Dressel with Coach Anthony Nesty (left) and Coach Steve Jungbluth (right)
Photos Courtesy of the University Athletic Association

Is there anything swimmers and coaches need to know about Coach Troy that they might not ever otherwise learn just from being around him on deck?

Caeleb: Well, he's a hard-ass. If you haven't made that clear in your book by now, you need to rewrite it. But, he's also one of the most selfless, caring people I've ever met. He's put his swimmers ahead of his family at times. He cares about us; it's not just a job for him, it's a craFort Troy wants to be a great coach, not just for himself but because he genuinely loves watching "unreal performances" from his swimmers. That's what makes it worth it for him.

He's all about those times and goals that weren't supposed to happen. He's there for people who are winning that weren't supposed to win but bought into him and what he is about. He likes to see swimmers *develop*. Not just swim fast, but the actual development of buying into something and putting all your energy and passion and full-on obsession with it to see it come through. He's not trying to take all the credit; he's not making money off of anyone succeeding; he just loves the development.

He's a special guy. He's really a big teddy bear. He's got such a hard reputation until you really get to know him. Yeah, his practices are *ridiculous*, but he's the same guy who can joke around and be your friend. He's a friend who cares about his swimmers and will hold you accountable to anything you put in front of him.

Leaving a Legacy

An integral part of being human is the desire to be noticed, known, and remembered. Most hope their families and friends remember them fondly and with positive memories. Men and women with greater ambitions have driven history with deeper passions and motives to be remembered for more. Coaches, by nature, want to help athletes achieve more than they believe possible of themselves. Some coaches touch hundreds of athletes' lives, some touch thousands. Some coaches guide athletes, who in turn inspire entire generations, some lead in a different manner, teaching other coaches how to hone their craFort

Beyond a coach's domain, be it a field, a pitch, a court, or a pool deck, coaches are involved in the betterment of their sports with the work they do in associations and governance. Coach Troy spent two years as the president of the American Swimming Coaches

Association, managing a wide range of issues concerning the sport of swimming at both the national and world levels. John Leonard, former Executive Director of the ASCA, had the following to say about Coach Troy's service to swimming as acting President:

Coach Gregg Troy was President of the American Swimming Coaches Association in 2013 and 2014, a period of intense growth in the Association in Membership, Services, and Certification.

Coach Troy brought a strong sense of urgency to the organization in terms of competitive success, concentration on 'what will make American Swimming better in performance' and a keen sense of how hard to push with the established powers at USA Swimming and FINA. A keen observer of all things in International Swimming, he was blessed with outstanding insight into how things would be decided and what the best pressure points were for changing what needed to be changed. He was also very skilled at being able to determine what the best thing to do 'NOW' was

Many of the same skills that made him a great coach, also made him a great leader for our Association.

Coach Troy can proudly say he's *helped in every possible fashion* as a coach. I asked Coach Troy, **"Coach, how do you want to be remembered? What do you want your legacy to be?"**

The initial off the cuff response probably sheds more light on Coach Troy's personality than anything else: "Honestly, from the swimming perspective...I don't give a damn." Clark Gable would have been proud of Coach Troy's reply.

After a few seconds of thought, "That's not to say I don't care, I just never thought about my career or passion for coaching in terms of awards or legacies. Number one: I hope everyone I have coached realizes how important family and children are. They are your most lasting impact on society. Number two: I'd like to hope I did something that impacted, not just the swimming community alone, but impacted people to use the skill sets they learned from swimming to become very effective in what they did the rest of their lives."

CONCLUSION

Saturday Morning, 2011

The buzzing energy in the air was a combination of frustration, panic, and passion. The University of Florida assistant coaches hustled from one corner of the pool to another, constantly giving feedback to athletes resting at the wall between repeats. The coaches yelled out finishing times as swimmers crashed into the two bulkhead at the middle of the indoor, 50-meter pool. Male swimmers were in the deep end of the Stephen C. O'Connell Center pool, while the women raced in the shallow end. The massive concrete rafters rise above the pool like a well-lit cathedral. This day, the athletes were finishing a "quality" set, a set designed to mimic racing tempos, intensity, and distances. Today's set was particularly brutal. Twelve sets of 100-yard repeats off the starting blocks on a big enough interval to catch your breath but not big enough for the lactate to clear the athlete's muscles. As that lactate builds up, pain does, too. Arms and legs seem to turn to concrete; hearts feel they're beating out of chests. The throbbing pain is excruciating and there is no respite, except the end of the set.

With only two repeats left, the set is all but done. Physically, everyone will finish. No one will pass out or be seriously maimed. Mentally, though? That's another story. Coach Troy's frustration *du jour* comes in the form of a freshman who is not used to this level of work. Coach's expectation for the set was for every single athlete to commit 100 percent to every repeat. Not one repeat was to be done with anything less than an all-out effort. While he had taken the time to explain the set beforehand, there were always athletes who held back and waited until the last few repeats to suddenly kick into gear and surge ahead.

Typical of younger age group swimmers and high school athletes, this particular freshman chose to hold back on the first 10 repeats, averaging :55 per 100 (six seconds off his best time). Coach Troy paced the deck and snarled at me, "Why can't these kids get it? Real results require real commitment. They have to be willing to hurt. That kid just won't hurt." I nodded and returned scribbling times on a clipboard of results I had been instructed to keep.

With my newly purchased stopwatch in one hand and the clipboard in another, I helped call out finishing times for one of the last lanes on the eleventh repeat as I heard him erupt from the bulkhead. Even over the music playing from the deck speakers, Coach's voice crashed like a hammer.

"What the hell are you doing?! How in God's name can you be dropping 3 seconds on the *second to last 100 of the set?!*" Apparently, the freshman's "save up" wasn't as impressive to Coach Troy as he thought it would be. "That nonsense works at a high school level, but if you're going to compete at NCAAs and be at your best *twice* in one day; you have to be ready to *hurt!*" As the tirade continued, coaches stopped what they were doing. Swimmers waited for the final send off. Several upperclassmen in the water had been on the receiving end of a challenge like this from Coach Troy in the past and were snickering behind their water bottles.

Coach Troy checked his watch to make sure the final interval send-off wasn't approaching anytime soon and continued to lambast the young man. The interval send-off approached quicker than Coach would have preferred, for which the freshman was duly thankful. He slinked off the wall as Coach Troy proceeded to follow him up and down the side of the pool. He paced with high-tempoed steps, nearly slipping on the wet deck several times. Arms swinging, stopwatch in hand, and whistling at the top of his lungs, Coach Troy put as much energy into encouraging and watching that 100 as the swimmer did racing it. At the final touch, the young man touched only one and a half seconds off his best time. Coach Troy burst into an animated stream of directives, and a unique mix of anger and pride in his voice drew the attention of everyone in the pool.

"*THAT'S* HOW YOU WERE SUPPOSED TO DO THE WHOLE SET! IF YOU'D BEEN WILLING TO DO THAT EARLIER, YOU'D BE WALKING OUT OF HERE A BETTER ATHLETE. AS IT IS, YOU'RE LEAVING THE SAME MEDIOCRE SWIMMER YOU WALKED IN."

While it wasn't true that he was a mediocre athlete, as the sheer acceptance on to the University of Florida team meant he was already at an exceptional level few would ever reach, Coach Troy's measured greatness on a wildly inflated scale. *Merely* going a time that would have won most states' high school State Championships in practice wasn't enough.

As coaches began reading out the warmdown set over individual lanes, Coach Troy stomped away and whispered to his assistant coach instructions to the effect of, "Check on him later and make sure he understands what happened." The intense gaze and animated hand gestures were clues that he was still fired up and excitable about the end of the set. I kept my eyes on the floor and tried to be as inconspicuous as possible; I'd hate to be caught in the path of the tropical storm that was Coach Troy.

I was scribbling down the last few times I needed from some finishing athletes when I noticed Coach Troy marching across the bulkhead heading my way. Strangely, he had a small smirk hiding behind the cup of ice he shook into his mouth. With the smallest of head shakes, he looked me in the eye and said, "It's never easy, Jackson." It took me a second to think—did he mean the set? Did he mean backstroke technique? Managing coaches? Motivating athletes?

"Coaching. This life. It's never easy. Are you sure you want this?" He stared at me, making me feel like I was a patient lying on a psychiatrist's couch. "Long days, constant irritations, pushing people who sometimes don't want to be pushed. It's. Never. Easy." Over his shoulder, I saw the young backstroker rising from the pool, laughing with his friends and being congratulated on his two impressive achievements: 1) completing a quality set with some remarkable times, and 2) surviving his first loud and in-your-face encounter with Coach Troy.

Was I sure? Was this life for me? Absolutely. I'd do anything to be able to inspire and drive the people around me to achieve the way Coach Troy did. People on the outside or casual observers look at Coach Troy and identify, "He's yelling and angry, that's the key to his coaching style." Such a shallow observation denies the decades

179

of work he's put in with athletes, learning how to best motivate and inspire athletes, either individually or as a group, and the follow up conversations that ensue between coach and athlete. Coach Troy's ability to tell hard truths directly to a person is a trait few can mimic. Winston Churchill once said, "A diplomat is a person who can tell you to go to hell in such a way that you actually look forward to the trip." While I don't think anyone, including his wife, would ever claim Coach Troy would make it as a diplomat, he *is* capable of telling someone the truth in a way that reaches them on a personal level and *inspires* them to make a change. Whether that change is made out of spite or out of self-interest is dependent on the offending athlete or coach. Either way, change comes from his truths.

To this day, every time I slump in my plush office chair and start to feel sorry for myself because of a hectic or discouraging day at work, I think about Coach Troy's words. *"It's never easy."* I compare my comfortable days to Coach Troy's early mornings and late nights in Fort Myers. I grapple with the idea of rebuilding a depleted boarding program and taking on new tasks for international federations. I marvel at the idea of shifting from Age Group club coaching to NCAA recruiting in a season; I dream about the glory and lights of the international stage underneath five colored rings on a white flag.

Unwilling to let Coach Troy down, even if he is thousands of miles away, I rise again and get back to being my best.

ACKNOWLEDGMENTS

First and foremost, I want to thank Coach Troy for allowing me to write this book. When I broached the idea with him, I fully expected him to say, "Biographies are for people who are dead." So, thank you, Coach Troy, for sharing your wisdom and stories and allowing me to put them to paper.

I want to thank Coach Chuck Warner for inspiring me to write this book, by writing such a great biography on Coach Eddie Reese that I was *compelled* to write the equivalent about my own mentor.

Thank you to Caeleb Dressel and Ryan Lochte for finding time to share your own Coach Troy insights. I know you didn't need distractions in the final months of Olympic prep, but this book wouldn't have been the same without your help.

As always, thank you, Mom and Dad, for your unwavering support and belief in me. I've always believed I could achieve anything I worked hard enough for; that's a belief you, as parents, taught me, and that grit can be traced directly to you two.

Thank you, Madeline, for putting up with edits at the dinner table and my half-listening replies. I love you.

Thank you, Paris Jacobs, for your brainstorming sessions and endless energy. Thank you, Coach Block, for your confidence I never feel I've truly earned. Thank you, Ana Castro, for the never-ending supply of coffee and help; and thank you to my swimmers, who constantly remind me to be better than the advice I offer them. Chloe and Jaime, thanks for your mad photoshop skills.

And finally, thank you to the coaches who won't get to read this. As I'm frequently reminded, "If we can see far, it's because we stand on the shoulders of giants."

Coach June Woolger

Coach Peter Daland

Coach Forbes Carlile

Coach Donnie Craine

APPENDIX

All-Americans @ NCAA Level

250+ individuals, 100+ relays

Gator Varsity Swimmers at the Olympics, 47 athletes representing 27 countries

USA- Beisel, Dressel, Dwyer, Lochte, Burckle

Spain- Costa Schmid, Solaeche-Gomez

Italy- D'Arrigo

Iceland- Luthersdottir, Bateman

New Zealand- C. Main

Colombia- Pinzón

South Africa- Rousseau, Townsend

Poland- Switkowski, Werner, Cieślak

US Virgin Islands- Rex Tullius

Great Britain- Dan Wallace, Loughran, Lowe, Proud, Spofforth

Barbados- Bradley Ally

Cayman Islands- B. Fraser, S. Fraser

Hungary- C. Gercsak, B. Gercsak, Rudolf

Tunisia- Lajnef

Puerto Rico- Martinez, Lopez

Canada- Russell, Sioui

Peru- Crescimbeni

Curacao- Davelaar

Venezuela- Gomez, Monasterio

Brazil- Mangabeira, Jayme
Estonia- Põld
Philippines- J.B. Walsh
Germany- Bernhardt
South Korea- Kim
Jamaica- Atkinson
Portugal- Laurentino
Barbados- Martindale

Bolles Swimmers → Olympics

14 Over 3 Olympiads representing 8 countries
1996
Carolyn Adel '96, Suriname
Casey Barrett '93, Canada
Gustavo Borges '91, Brazil
Greg Burgess '90, United States
Claudia Franco '93, Spain
Dominik Galic '94, Croatia
Cerian Gibbes '00, Trinidad and Tobago
Trina Jackson '95, United States
Ashley Whitney '98, United States
Martin Zubero '87, Spain

1992
Gustavo Borges '91, Brazil
Greg Burgess '90, United States
Jose De Souza '89, Brazil
Giovanni Linscheer '90, Suriname
Anthony Nesty '87, Suriname

Patrick Sagisi '89, Guam

Martin Zubero '87, Spain

1988

Anthony Nesty '87, Suriname

Patrick Sagisi '89, Guam

Martin Zubero '87, Spain

Major International Meets

Medalist in each event except the 100m Breaststroke and 200m Breaststroke

50 Free- Dressel

100 Free- Dressel

200 Free- Lochte

400 Free- Vanderkaay

800/1500 Free- Atkinson

100 Fly- Dressel

200 Fly- Rousseau

100 Backstroke- Spofforth

200 Backstroke- Beisel, Lochte

200 IM- Lochte

400 IM- Beisel, Lochte

400 Free Relay- Lochte

800 Free Relay- Lochte

400 Medley Relay- Lochte

Florida Gators- SEC and NCAA Finishes Women

Year	SEC	NCAA
1997	5th	20th
1998	3rd	15th
1999	4th	8th
2000	3rd	19th
2001	3rd	8th
2002	1st	4th
2003	2nd	6th
2004	3rd	4th
2005	3rd	4th
2006	3rd	10th
2007	3rd	7th
2008	2nd	6th
2009	1st	7th
2010	2nd	1st
2011	2nd	7th
2012	3rd	10th
2013	3rd	6th
2014	3rd	6th
2015	3rd	9th
2016	6th	19th
2017	7th	X
2018	7th	35th

Florida Gators - SEC and NCAA Finishes
Men

Year	SEC	NCAA
1998	4th	26th
1999	4th	17th
2000	2nd	9th
2001	3rd	5th
2002	2nd	4th
2003	2nd	6th
2004	2nd	6th
2005	2nd	5th
2006	2nd	5th
2007	2nd	4th
2008	2nd	8th
2009	2nd	5th
2010	2nd	5th
2011	2nd	5th
2012	2nd	8th
2013	1st	6th
2014	1st	3rd
2015	1st	5th
2016	1st	3rd
2017	1st	3rd
2018	1st	5th

ABOUT THE AUTHOR

Jackson Leonard has been involved with swimming at every level of the sport, from teaching Learn to Swim lessons to coaching NCAA qualifiers. After being mentored by University of Florida greats: Martyn Wilby, Anthony Nesty, and Gregg Troy, Jackson has coached Age Group Champions, Zone Record Holders, Junior and Senior National Qualifiers, National Age Group Record Holders, State Champions, NCAA Qualifiers and more.

Jackson received his Master's Degree in Education from the University of Florida in 2015 and is currently working toward his Doctorate in Education in Leadership and Innovation. Aside from the wet side of club coaching, he enjoys running and reading.

Printed in the USA
CPSIA information can be obtained
at www.ICGtesting.com
LVHW020721231223
767291LV00070B/982